Semantic Acquisition Games

Jakub Šimko · Mária Bieliková

Semantic Acquisition Games

Harnessing Manpower for Creating Semantics

 Springer

Jakub Šimko
Mária Bieliková
Institute of Informatics and Software
  Engineering
Slovak University of Technology
Bratislava
Slovakia

ISBN 978-3-319-06114-6   ISBN 978-3-319-06115-3   (eBook)
DOI 10.1007/978-3-319-06115-3
Springer Cham Heidelberg New York Dordrecht London

Library of Congress Control Number: 2014935974

Printed on acid-free paper

Springer is part of Springer Science+Business Media (www.springer.com)

Acknowledgments

This book originated from research carried out at the Institute of Informatics and Software Engineering of the Faculty of Informatics and Information Technologies of Slovak University of Technology in Bratislava. It was partially supported by several research projects for more than a period of 3 years. The majority of this book is based on the results of the dissertation project submitted by the first author.

Several individuals have directly or indirectly influenced this research and thus helped in shaping the content of this book. We would like to thank our colleagues at the Institute for their patience, advice and support during research that shaped this book, be it discussions or simply a help in realizing numerous experiments presented in this book. We would especially like to thank Dr. Michal Tvarožek for his extensive advice, critical to many aspects of this work. Special thanks also go to Balázs Nagy and Peter Dulačka, students who made many of the experiments possible. We also wish to thank all the members of the Personalized Web (PeWe, pewe.fiit.stuba.sk) research group for their enthusiastic participation in experiments and for providing us with valuable feedback.

We also wish to thank the reviewers for their valuable feedback, enabling us to improve the book in various ways and Springer and its editors for making the publication possible.

Contents

Chapter 1
Introduction

Abstract With the ever-lasting need for semantics and metadata to describe the resources (not only) on the Web, the focus is brought to the human-centered approaches to semantics acquisition. Within them, inherent to the crowdsourcing, a specific group of approaches, the semantics acquisition games (SAGs) have emerged in the last decade. The SAGs deserve the researchers' attention, as they provide cheap means of motivation of human workers to perform semantics acquisition jobs. The goals of our work, outlined in this chapter, are oriented towards creation of new SAG-based approaches and contributing with reusable SAG design principles. The book also aims to provide a comprehensive review of the field of semantics acquisition games and their design principles.

Nowadays, the amount of information on the Web grows fast [11]. In order to be able to search the Web and utilize its content, we require meta-information about individual resources (the resource metadata), especially describing the semantic meaning of resource contents (the resource semantics). In opposite to the heterogeneity of web resources (e.g., texts, web pages, multimedia, applications), metadata must be homogeneous in order to be easily processed by machines. Due to the scale and growing speed of the Web, the approaches for the metadata acquisition must be scalable (to cover the large space of resources) and precise (to provide quality metadata that would not mislead their users).

The Semantic Web was envisioned as a future form of Web, which (in addition to human-readable resources) would offer a machine readable representation of the information and knowledge contained within its resources. The Semantic Web can be seen as a meta-layer of the "common" Web: a collection of web resource description unified under universal and widely accepted domain models using the unified representation (the Semantic Web is split in two main parts: the *core semantics* (or *domain models*) usually represented as ontologies and *resource descriptions* kept as parts of the resources themselves (e.g. HTML meta-tags) or in separate repositories). The provisions of such corpora would be tremendous. Apart from solving complex queries [11, 18], it would be much more easier to solve the problem of (web) information space invisibility [9], which describes the situations, where users are unable

J. Šimko and M. Bieliková, *Semantic Acquisition Games*,
DOI: 10.1007/978-3-319-06115-3_1,
© Springer International Publishing Switzerland 2014

to come up with good-enough search queries to satisfy their needs (usually, this happens when users are not familiar with the domain they are searching). In such situations, the Semantic Web would allow to create easy-to-browse information space abstractions that help the searchers to orient themselves within the domain they are not familiar with.

Unfortunately the vision is far from the fulfillment. The Semantic Web does not exists in the scale needed to become a background for a prevailing search paradigm (although we can observe promising initiatives such as linked data creation [1]). The reason is that creation of proper web resource metadata requires human expertise and extensive work (which may go costly in web scale) or sophisticated automated methods doing the same job (which have presently only limited capabilities). Extensive effort is also needed to create the domain models (to cover the layer from the top) either by manual means or in devising automated methods. This makes the semantics acquisition an attractive field with a plethora of existing approaches and research opportunities.

We roughly split the existing approaches to semantics acquisition into the following categories (although they also tend to overlap and complement each other):

1. *Expert (human computation) work.* Comprises work of domain experts, who create either annotations of resources or domain ontologies (e.g., project Cyc [8]). They may also include other approaches where metadata are created with expertise of a single individual. Manual semantics creation delivers high quality results, but cannot cover the vastness of the Web without being too expensive.
2. *Crowd (human computation) work—the crowdsourcing* is still human-originating semantics creation, but capable of delivering semantics in high quantity, although with quality varying in terms of generality (they do not work well in specialized domains). The "crowd" means that there are many knowledge-contributing individuals in the process. This is usually possible thanks to the fact that crowd members contribute only as a by-product of other primary activity they are motivated to do (e.g., contributing image annotations while organizing their image galleries). The second reason is that crowd members are "non-experts" regarding the (semantics acquisition) job they perform. To keep quality outputs in these conditions, several validation mechanisms are being used, for example multiple user agreement [2, 13]. The general crowdsourcing also includes game-based approaches, i.e. *crowdsourcing games* (sometimes called *games with a purpose* [20])—specially designed games that transform work-like tasks to entertaining experiences. When we use crowdsourcing games for semantics acquisition, we call them *semantics acquisition games* (SAGs). The field of SAGs is the primary field of interest of this work.
3. *Machine (automated) approaches* for semantics acquisition implement various natural language processing techniques, data mining and machine learning in order to annotate resources or extract domain knowledge [6, 12, 14, 16, 21]. While capable of delivering even web scale quantity of information, they often suffer from inaccuracies, mainly due to the heterogeneous nature of the Web and natural language, which they cannot effectively sustain. Nevertheless, they are

effectively being deployed to narrow problems, where enough training data is available or when they can be supervised by humans effectively.

The *crowdsourcing games* established themselves over the last decade as powerful means of harnessing of the human computational capacity and also as a research field [7, 19, 20]. They take the advantage of the fact that computer game players do non-trivial thinking during gaming in order to win: they formulate strategies, evaluate complex situations, make decisions or consume and process the multimedia content. Crowdsourcing games aim to harness this actual brain power in their favor. Using a specially designed game rules, they align the game process and winning conditions with solving a *human intelligence task*—a task that is easy to be solved by a human being, but hard or impossible to be done by a machine [5, 10, 15]. Crowdsourcing games record played games and use these logs to extract portions of knowledge produced by the players, further cross-validating them in order to retrieve problem solutions and useful virtual artifacts.

Many of the crowdsourcing games are used for (web) semantics acquisition tasks—we then call them *semantics acquisition games* (SAGs). These tasks predominately include:

- **Acquisition of multimedia annotations.** Here, the games are designed in a way that players need to provide information about multimedia in order to win [17]. A prominent example is the *ESP Game*, where two players collect points when they match on a particular textual description of a given image [5, 20].
- **Acquisition of text annotations.** Some SAGs were devised for tasks in natural language processing, namely the co-reference matching [3, 4].
- **Acquisition of domain models.** Variety of games was designed for ontology construction, like common fact collecting [20], ontology expansion [7, 10] or ontology linking [19].

Altogether, the semantics acquisition games represent an attractive research field as they may be potentially used for many human intelligence tasks. But apart from fulfilling individual purposes, the SAGs impose also some general design challenges that have not yet been solved: lack of effective validation of created artifacts (i.e. the "useful" products of the game), anti-cheating issues, lack of popularity and attractiveness [7, 20]. Today SAGs are being created ad-hoc for each human intelligence task, and there is no generic methodology for straightforward transformation of a problem to a game, which leaves very interesting research questions open.

1.1 Challenges and Goals

Our work is aligned around the domain of human oriented approaches to semantics acquisition: the semantics acquisition games (SAGs) which are established as a part of crowdsourcing (resp. human computation) research field. From the semantics acquisition standpoint, there are several, still-open challenges.

There is still a lack of sufficient semantics for domain models, especially in specialized domains (as opposite to the well establishing general domain models of linked data). The ever increasing number of multimedia resources (images, music) is not covered with sufficient descriptive metadata creation (in both quantity and quality). In connection to the above, the SAG approaches have trouble to solve more specific human intelligence tasks for which only small groups of sufficiently experienced players are usually available. Based on these challenges, we formulated our first goal:

> Goal 1: Add to semantics acquisition with new effective and functioning, SAG-based approaches and, if possible, for specific domains, where the lack of the semantics is more severe and where only limited number of players is available.

Secondly, our work orients itself on the state-of-the-art of the *design* of the semantics acquisition games and names its main open challenges.

The SAG design and development is a non-trivial task and there is only a little of existing guidance on how to create these games. The SAGs are created ad-hoc and have to deal with cold-start problems (or they fail to provide feedback to the players according to the quality of artifacts they are producing), popularity (the games look more or less like a work) and player cheating problems (which hamper not only the fairness of the game but also damages their "useful" output value). Thus, a major challenge for researchers is to come up with a complex methodology for SAG design.

Validation schemes for player-created artifacts (such as synchronous consensus of the crowd), which SAGs use for ensuring the quality of their output, are not sufficient in acquisition of correct solutions for human intelligence tasks that require certain degree of expertise of the workers. Even if there is a minority of experts in the crowd, their voice is "overrun" by the lay majority. The research challenge is therefore to *identify experts and authorities* within the crowd of players, and assign them with more voting power. Based on these challenges, we formulate our second goal:

> Goal 2: Improve the effectiveness of semantics acquisition games by developing design principles, independent on the problem domain, which the SAG is dealing with. In particular, we focus on the possibilities of
>
> 1. reducing the cold start problems of SAGs,
> 2. preventing malicious player behavior and
> 3. taking advantage of players with more expertise and confidence for solving the game's purpose.

1.2 Book Outline

This book is split into two major parts to cover our two goals. The part one covers our work with semantics acquisition games from the perspective of semantics acquisition. It focuses on the state-of-the-art in semantics acquisition in general (expert-based, automated and crowd-based approaches) and for semantics acquisition games. After, it presents design and evaluation our own SAG-based methods. The part two of the book is oriented to the problem areas of designing the SAGs. It first reviews the field of SAGs from this point of view, introducing a design aspect classification of SAGs. Next, it projects our own SAGs through this perspective, pointing out several novel design patterns and approaches.

Part one contains chapters as follows:

- Chapter 2 (State-of-the-art: semantics acquisition and crowdsourcing) reviews the trends in semantics acquisition approaches, moving through expert and automated approaches to crowdsourcing, which represents a broader domain of our research.
- Chapter 3 (State-of-the-art: semantics acquisition games) reviews the existing crowdsourcing games and semantics acquisition games by type of the semantics acquisition job they perform.
- Chapter 4 (Little Search Game: a method for lightweight domain modeling) presents and evaluates two games that utilize principles of negative search to assess term relationships.
- Chapter 5 (PexAce: a method for image metadata acquisition) presents and evaluates a card game through which image tags are collected. We also present a game's modification for acquisition of metadata for personal imagery.
- Chapter 6 (CityLights: a method for music metadata validation) presents and evaluates a question-based SAG, where player behavior indicates the validity of existing music metadata.

The part two contains chapters as follows:

- Chapter 7 (State-of-the-art: design of the semantics acquisition games) reviews the current trends and problems universal for SAG design, presents our SAG design classification.
- Chapter 8 (Our SAGs: design aspects and improvements) looks at our own SAGs presented in part one, but from the design perspectives. In particular, it points out novel methods and "design patterns" for cold-start problem reduction, cheating detection and player expertise and confidence exploitation, introduced by our games that can be generalized for use elsewhere.

We then conclude the book and turn back to the crowdsourcing and reflect several of our findings on this broader domain. We also points out future challenges for crowdsourcing and semantics acquisition games.

References

1. Bizer, C., Heath, T., Berners-Lee, T.: Linked data—the story so far. Int. J. Semantic Web Inf. Syst. **5**(3), 1–22 (2009)
2. Bizer, C., Lehmann, J., Kobilarov, G., Auer, S., Becker, C., Cyganiak, R., Hellmann, S.: Dbpedia—a crystallization point for the web of data. Web Semant. **7**, 154–165 (2009)

3. Chamberlain, J., Poesio, M., Kruschwitz, U.: A demonstration of human computation using the phrase detectives annotation game. In: Proceedings of the ACM SIGKDD W. on Human Computation, HCOMP'09, pp. 23–24. ACM, New York, NY, USA (2009) NULL

4. Hladka, B., Mirovsky, J., Schlesinger, P.: Designing a language game for collecting coreference annotation. In: Proceedings of the Third Linguistic Annotation W., pp. 52–55. Association for, Computational Linguistics (2009)

5. Ho, C.J., Chang, T.H., Lee, J.C., Hsu, J.Y.j., Chen, K.T.: Kisskissban: a competitive human computation game for image annotation. In: Proceedings of the ACM SIGKDD W. on Human Computation, HCOMP'09, pp. 11–14. ACM, New York, NY, USA (2009)

6. Kozareva, Z.: Bootstrapping named entity recognition with automatically generated gazetteer lists. In: Proceedings of the Eleventh Conf. of the European Chapter of the Association for Computational Linguistics: Student Research W. on - EACL'06, pp. 15–21. Association for Computational Linguistics, Morristown, NJ, USA (2006)

7. Krause, M., Takhtamysheva, A., Wittstock, M., Malaka, R.: Frontiers of a paradigm: exploring human computation with digital games. In: Proceedings of the ACM SIGKDD W. on Human Computation, HCOMP'10, pp. 22–25. ACM, New York, NY, USA (2010)

8. Lenat, D.B.: CYC: a large-scale investment in knowledge infrastructure. Commun. ACM **38**(11), 33–38 (1995)

9. Marchionini, G.: From finding to understanding. Commun. ACM **49**(4), 41–46 (2006)

10. Markotschi, T., Völker, J.: GuessWhat?! Human Intelligence for Mining Linked Data. Proceedings of the W. on Knowledge Injection into and Extraction from Linked Data (KIELD) at the International Conference on Knowledge Engineering and Knowledge Management (EKAW), pp. 1–12 (2010)

11. Marmanis, H., Babenko, D.: Algorithms of the Intelligent Web, 1st edn. Manning Publications Co., Greenwich (2009)

12. Mcdowell, L., Cafarella, M.: Ontology-driven, unsupervised instance population. Web Semanti. Sci. Serv. Agents World Wide Web **6**(3), 218–236 (2008)

13. Mullins, M., Fizzano, P.: Treelicious: a system for semantically navigating tagged web pages. In: Web Intelligence and Intelligent Agent Technology, IEEE/WIC/ACM International Conference, pp. 91–96 (2010)

14. Pantel, P., Pennacchiotti, M.: Automatically harvesting and ontologizing semantic relations. In Proceeding of the 2008 Conference on Ontology Learning and Population: Bridging the Gap between Text and Knowledge, pp. 171–195. IOS Press, Amsterdam, The Netherlands (2008)

15. Roman, D.: Crowdsourcing and the question of expertise. Commun. ACM **52**, 12–12 (2009)

16. Sanchez, D., Moreno, A.: Learning non-taxonomic relationships from web documents for domain ontology construction. Data Knowl. Eng. **64**(3), 600–623 (2008)

17. Seneviratne, L., Izquierdo, E.: An interactive framework for image annotation through gaming. In: Proceedings of the International Conference on Multimedia Information Retrieval, MIR'10, pp. 517–526. ACM, New York, NY, USA (2010)

18. Shadbolt, N., Berners-Lee, T., Hall, W.: The semantic web revisited. IEEE Intell. Syst. **21**, 96–101 (2006)

19. Siorpaes, K., Hepp, M.: Games with a purpose for the semantic web. IEEE Intell. Syst. **23**, 50–60 (2008)

20. von Ahn, L., Dabbish, L.: Designing games with a purpose. Commun. ACM **51**(8), 58–67 (2008)

21. Weichselbraun, A., Wohlgenannt, G., Scharl, A.: Refining non-taxonomic relation labels with external structured data to support ontology learning. Data Knowl. Eng. **69**(8), 763–778 (2010)

Part I
Games for Semantics Acquisition

Chapter 2
State-of-the-Art: Semantics Acquisition and Crowdsourcing

Abstract In this chapter we review the field of semantics acquisition to provide ground for further discussion on the semantics acquisition games. First, we cover the necessary definitions and review the main "client" approaches for semantics utilization—the information retrieval applications. Then, we move through three major groups of semantics acquisition approaches. The first group constitutes the expert-based approaches: costly, yet often essential for certain tasks such as seeding, setting-up schemas and semantics acquisition output validation. As second, we review the automated approaches: quantitatively effective, yet with questionable quality of output, widely utilized for many tasks such as ontology learning or resource metadata acquisition. Finally, we review the crowd-based approaches, which represent a balance between quality and quantity. They comprise many working schemes, ranging from "explicit" mechanical turking, to "implicit" social tagging applications and of course semantics acquisition games.

2.1 Semantics: Forms and Standards

In general, the term semantics stands for "meaning" and has many interpretations depending on the domain it is used in (e.g., philosophy, linguistics, programming). In the web science field it stands for a formally and explicitly represented meaning of resources (of the Web) readable and "understandable" by machines. At first look, such definition covers only the direct descriptions of resources (such as tags describing an image), however, in practical use, it covers also "not-so-direct", formally expressed facts, which are also part of meta-information layer above the Web, the domain models (which define the axioms and facts about the world they model). In our work, we use this broader definition. The *web* semantics is then the whole layer of semantics above the web resources. The Semantic Web is its subset that uses specific formalisms, which are widely accepted in the community as semantics representation. The semantics comes in different flavors according to their representations and also

J. Šimko and M. Bieliková, *Semantic Acquisition Games*,
DOI: 10.1007/978-3-319-06115-3_2,
© Springer International Publishing Switzerland 2014

their use. In our work, we recognize two major types: the core semantics (domain models) and resource descriptions (also referred as annotations or resource metadata).

The core of the Semantic Web are the ontologies, which model the *domain knowledge*: the common facts of the world (e.g., "carnivorous animals eat animals"), abstract or concrete concept definitions (e.g., "mammal is an animal") or constraints and rules of the world (e.g., "mammals have between 2 or 4 legs"). Ontologies are the world abstraction and represent an worldwide agreement on domain's general rules.

Ontologies that are highly structured and elaborated are often called the "heavyweight" semantics. Though they provide advanced capabilities, they are also hard to obtain and are almost exclusively built by (costly) human experts. The cheaper and more easy-to-create are the "lightweight" semantics with "lightweight" representations. These include *taxonomies* (hierarchical organizations of entities) and free association networks (which express general relatedness of entities) sometimes referred to as *folksonomies* (in case they were created using a crowdsourcing technique). The semantic structures sometimes use simple terms instead of concepts (also due to ease of creation), which of course, brings drawbacks like semantic ambiguity.

The prevailing standards for ontology representation are RDF (resource description framework) and OWL (web ontology language). The basic elements of ontologies are atomic facts expressed in the form of *triplets* consisting of the source and target entity (*subject* and *object*) connected with a *predicate* (e.g., "dog" (subject)—"is a" (predicate)—"mammal" (object)). Triplets represent various types of relationships among entities (e.g., hierarchy, composition, usage). Each entity or predicate has a textual description, but also URI that identifies it globally. The ontology entities represent *concepts* (classes) or their instances. Each entity can also be decorated with literal properties. Using these basic elements, more complex facts are composed.

As second part of the Semantic Web, *resource descriptions* are the connection between the domain models and web resources. For example, they may denote to which particular concepts the resources are related (e.g., "this article is about bears") or they provide additional structural information about particular document (e.g., document outline based on semantic properties of individual paragraphs).

Resource annotations are represented either in the knowledge bases (e.g., as RDF triplets) or as a direct part of the web resources itself (e.g., meta-tags of HTML, RDFa). They also vary in terms of what kind of resource (or its part) they annotate. Different kinds of annotations are found in case of texts (the annotation can be related to whole text, paragraph, sentence or even single word), images (spatial information), audio tracks or videos (temporal information).

2.2 Semantics in Use

The web semantics is utilized in various applications. Typically, they are connected to the information retrieval, information space organization, navigation or recommender systems.

Since only a fraction of the Web is covered with descriptive semantics, the applications utilizing them are also limited. Typically, a "semantic application" is dedicated to some specific corpus (e.g., an e-shop search and navigation supported by product descriptions). Heavyweight semantics are not common—applications rely more on lightweight semantics (e.g., product taxonomies).

Today, the query-based search fueled by keyword indexing approaches represents a dominant information retrieval paradigm. A majority of Web users utilize it as their primary way to satisfy their information needs. It also has many drawbacks: expressiveness limits [14], keyword ambiguity [36], invisibility of information space [44], just to mention a few. To solve these issues, some researchers and practitioners suggest a radical change of search paradigm (e.g., exploratory search), others argue for solutions that would not disturb the user who is unwilling to change his keyword search habits (e.g., result re-ranking, query expansion). Though, almost all alternatives somehow rely on semantics.

2.2.1 Query-Based Search

An example of the use of semantics for improving keyword-based search is solving a problem of *term meaning disambiguation* [33]. Searchers utilizing keyword search often encounter problem with homonyms used in the query—their result set gets spoiled with irrelevant (from their perspective) results, because the search terms have multiple meanings. Not all users are able to overcome such issues by themselves.

Researches employed different strategies for solving the search term ambiguity issue. The utilization of semantics plays a vital role in them. Köhler et al. [33] used existing ontologies to index a corpus of websites. They disambiguated terms within the websites using term relationships from the ontologies and were therefore able to infer related concepts, not just keywords. Using the same strategy for search queries, they were able to match relevant search results more accurately.

Another approach to term disambiguation implements the modeling of the searcher. The idea is to track the user's desires, long term interests or context, represent it in a formal model and measure its relatedness to the potential search results either by query enhancements or result filtering. Comparison is used to re-rank the results, so they satisfy the searcher. Though some researchers [6, 36] attempt to do it on the syntactical (keyword) level, much better results were achieved, if the user and resources were modeled using "heavier" semantics [5].

The search query expansion approaches [4, 9] directly involve searcher's actions in query disambiguation. Normally, when searcher formulates an ambiguous query, he tries to reformulate it by introducing other keywords, if he can think of any. The point of query-expansion approaches is to aid him with this by recommending a possible search terms to append to the query and to refine the search. Prior to this, a domain model is required to provide relationships of terms in the original query, to other possible search terms.

2.2.2 *Exploratory Search*

In 2006, Gary Marchionini coined the term *exploratory search* and marked the birth of a new search paradigm, which tried to solve the problems with invisibility of the Web [44]. The invisibility problem is often formulated as the inability of the Web user (searcher) to formulate a search query in a particular domain, because of a lack of familiarity with domain's jargon and structure (it can also be observed in the above case of ambiguous query reformulation).

Marchionini states that not all web search tasks are sufficiently solvable by keyword search, namely learning and information composition tasks. He also states the problems of inexperienced users new to certain domains, who do not know the domain jargon and are thus unable to type in proper keywords [44]. Marchionini suggests the use of alternative search interfaces that visualize some abstraction of the domain that user can afterward navigate and filter the content rather by browsing, then by query formulation. However realization of such interface requires a suitable semantics: both resource descriptions and domain models.

A very basic example of an exploratory search tool is a tag cloud. A relatively widespread technique for result filtering visualizes an information space as a collection of words which characterize its content—the individual resources. The words are usually displayed to the searcher in different sizes reflecting their weight (e.g., importance, frequency) in the corpus. The user is then allowed to review the cloud, learn about the contents of the otherwise invisible corpus. Moreover, he can interact with the cloud by selecting its individual words to filter the result set.

Usually, tag clouds operate over keywords assigned to the resources. However, they could be used with more elaborate semantics too. One example of an search and navigation application exploiting ontologies in this way is *Idea Navigation* [63]. With simply looking textual interface, it directly uses the triplets (instead of tags) to propose possible options of filtering the result set to users. This allows the searcher to learn more about the domain he is reviewing.

A much more elaborate example of exploratory search approach is a faceted browser which heavily relies on semantics. One of such named *Factic* was created by Tvarožek and Bieliková [67, 68]. The faceted browser is an information retrieval application that uses facets (a filter criteria along with their possible values) as the means of formulating of the search queries (rather then by typed-in keywords). Faceted browsers are typical in e-shops where the visitor can filter the products by their parameters (in Factic, the facets are even generated automatically based on metadata in ontological repository to which it is attached). The provision of such approach is apparent, the customer can immediately see what is available and he already has a good overview of the whole information space on the e-shop portal, because he sees the category structure and also a list of faceted criteria and their possible values. This, of course, depends on well devised ontology or at least set of homogeneous resource descriptions.

2.2.3 Creation is the Harder Part

Though we have not covered other fields where semantics are used like recommender systems [34] or learning frameworks [8], we have illustrated the important role of semantics in today's Web applications. Many of them still await the "critical mass" of existing web semantics in sufficient quality. We have seen that they do not need a particularly rich (heavyweight) semantics to work. Nevertheless, even the light-weight semantics is not available in sufficient scale.

Regardless on how the semantics are used or which type of resource they describe, their creation usually represent the harder part in the job of semantics-based applications development. Many research works (including this) are devoted solely to this task, leaving the semantics use to others. We now continue in description of the existing approaches to semantics creation, which can be split into three categories: manual, automated and crowd-based.

2.3 Manual (Expert-Based) Approaches

Manual approaches for building semantics rely on individual (or small groups of) experts, who create domain models or resource descriptions. Because of the dedicated human work, controlled environment and expertise the experts produce high quality semantics. Their capabilities are, however, limited quantitatively. Employing an expert in a specialized domain can be very costly. Additionally, experts need to be trained to understand the concept, representation and tools for semantics definition (in this task, they are sometimes aided with software tools [28]).

Expert work is essential for certain types of semantics acquisition tasks. In ontology engineering, experts are needed for correct definition of the top layers of the concept (class) hierarchy and system of ontology predicates and constraints. Another example is creation of gold standard datasets or "grand truths" used in evaluation of other semantics acquisition approaches.

The ontology engineering represents a field of study of creating ontologies and covers the spectrum of manual (expert) domain model creation approaches. It covers a variety of methods and methodologies comprising (not only):

- Strategies for defining relevant domain concepts [30].
- Methodologies for definition of relationship schema and ontology axioms [20]—a step which greatly influences the expressiveness of the ontology and the capabilities of automated inference over the ontology.
- Specialized methods for improving collaboration among experts during the ontology building [43, 48].
- What strategies to use in ontology mapping (i.e. interlinking multiple ontologies)—a task which mostly involves seeking for equivalent concepts within different ontologies [32].

- How to clean existing ontologies. Realizing repetitive problems and mistakes occurring during the ontology building, some researchers came up with sets of guidelines for clearing inconsistencies within ontologies [27].

The physical creation of the ontology is then done through software tools like Protégé[1] (WebProtégé [66]) or HOZO [47].

Experts are also employed in resource description acquisition tasks, mostly for commercial purposes. Typical examples are photography, 2D textures or press agency databases. Usually, such corpora are not freely available to public (paid services for professionals, e.g., journalists, designers) and do not follow the description standards of the Semantic Web (i.e. using standards like RDF and linking to global ontologies). However, the principles that are used there are similar to those on of the Semantic Web and such corpora could be eventually (straightforwardly) transformed to meet the Semantic Web standards.

Quantity of delivered semantics is the major disadvantage of expert-based semantics acquisition approaches. However, even manually created knowledge base can grow in size, if it is given enough time and effort. In the *Cyc* project,[2] a general knowledge base has been constructed for 25 years [38]. The project is being developed for commercial purposes (to be utilized, for example, by expert systems), but it has also been made partially published through the *OpenCyc* release—which demonstrated the impressive scale of 47 thousands of concepts and 306 thousands of facts (triplets or property assignments). Other positive aspect of the Cyc is its exhaustiveness: it covers—at least on top levels of abstraction—the whole spectrum of human knowledge. Another advantage is the inclusion of common sense facts that are not present in a written form, simply because they are commonly known (e.g., "You cannot remember events that have not happened yet.").

The Cyc knowledge base is heavyweight: it is highly structured and provides also a reasoning engine to answer even complex logical questions. This, however, comes with a price: the eventual volunteer effort to contribute new facts or even the usage of the knowledge base becomes a difficult task due to its complexity. The Cyc critics also note numerous gaps in the ontology: while there is enough concepts the relevant relationships among them often miss [72]. But even with these drawbacks, the Cyc knowledge base is usable and expandable and can be a good benchmark for evaluation of automated semantics acquisition approaches.

Another good example of expertly created knowledge base is the *WordNet*[3] dictionary [24], used by many web semantics projects. Created and maintained at Princeton university since 1985, it contains English language words organized by *synsets* (according to their synonymic relatedness), parts of speech, lexemes (various textual forms of the same term) and other relationships (e.g., hypernyms, holonyms). In comparison to Cyc, WordNet is a lightweight corpus. It operates over words, not concepts. Its set of relationships between words is limited and very abstract. Axioms,

---

[1] http://protege.stanford.edu/

[2] http://www.cyc.com/

[3] http://wordnet.princeton.edu/

constraints or literal attributes absent in its structures. This, naturally, reduces the options of its utilization. On the other hand, its upkeep becomes much more cheaper.

Both Cyc and WordNet are examples of originally "old" (1980) initiatives of domain modeling efforts surviving to this day. They have been created before the birth of the Web. When the idea of Semantic Web emerged, it firstly plead for creation of yet another all-covering (web) world model. However, it soon became apparent that such knowledge base could not be maintained centrally.

This problem was answered with Linked Data initiative. The Linked (Open) Data represent a system of interlinked resources, facts and vocabularies grouped into ontologies, each specialized to a specific domain [11]. Linked Data are, in general, lightweight: their common knowledge representation framework is RDF. This is one of reasons of Linked Data proliferation: the contribution of knowledge to such structure is easier than with heavyweight ontologies. Smaller specialized domain models are easier to maintain. The individual ontologies of the Linked Data overlap which yields a plethora of equivalence relationships between them. Linked Data also incorporated older knowledge bases and reached almost universal recognition in the community as a de-facto central entity of the today's Semantic Web.

2.4 Automated Approaches

Automated approaches to semantics acquisition rely on extraction of facts out of existing (electronic) human-readable knowledge bases. They have been subjects to many research activities, mainly because they do not rely on cooperation with human contributors which are problematically motivated (for cutting them off, these approaches provide much better scalability). Automated approaches can be seen from several points of view:

- **The source corpora and domain**. The corpus that can be mined can be the whole Web, or it's subset. It can also be a closed repository of documents (usually related to some domain). Generally, reduction of the input corpus naturally influences the quantity (and also quality) of acquired facts, helps in dealing with the heterogeneity of the resources and brings possibilities to exploit repetitive structures established within the corpus (e.g., reducing corpus to Wikipedia brings the advantages of the infoboxes, which contain structured data).
- **The degree of supervision**, or amount of expert knowledge needed to fuel the process. The typical example of supervised approach is a text mining algorithm, looking for occurrence of certain predefined phrase pattern(s) (e.g., "such as"). On the other side, an unsupervised approach example is the latent semantic analysis of texts (mining frequent term collocations). In general, supervised approaches usually provide better precision, while the unsupervised ones may process more heterogeneous inputs with unexpected situations.
- The **type of job** they do. In ontology building, approaches focus on concept identification, concept instance discovery or on relationship discovery which is

further split by the types of relationship they are able to provide (e.g., non-named, taxonomic or typed). Some approaches are dedicated on relationship naming (which is relevant for example when structuring the lightweight semantics). In resource description acquisition, the approaches can be classified by type of resource they aim to describe: texts, web pages, images, music, videos, etc.

2.4.1 Entity Recognition, Instance Population

When extracting facts from natural language text corpora, the first task for the extraction method is to identify the relevant entities, which will take part as subjects and objects of the triplets. These entities are directly mentioned in the analyzed text. Although, we can imagine that the list of entities (concepts or instances) related to a certain textual resource is possibly wider than the list of "meaningful" lexical units actually present in the text. E.g., there is an article about the American president, without the actual presence of lexical units "American" and "president" in it.

Before entity recognition, the text is usually preprocessed by tokenization and lemmatization (or stemming is used) producing basic morph *terms* (or stems). Then, the stopwords are removed. These are usually supportive words carrying no semantic meaning (e.g., prepositions). The stopwords sometimes contain meaningful words too—in cases they are very frequent in the corpus and thus cannot be used to distinct between resources.

After the preprocessing, the entities are selected, depending on the method. A relatively naive approach is the selection of terms belonging to noun part of speech (which are identified using a dictionary like WordNet). In case of named entity recognition, capitalized terms are selected. Some entity recognition algorithms also solve the possible polysemy (multiple meanings of the same lexemes) of terms, for example by exploiting the existing concept collocation database or thesaurus [46].

Note that the *named entities* require quite different approach for identification. They comprise personal and company names, shortcuts, geographical locations, etc. They are usually not present in the dictionaries. Some approaches for named entity recognition rely on building extensive datasets of such names, which do not have to be necessarily manually created. As example, we can take gazetteer lists constructed by machine learning in the work of Kozareva [35]. A particular problem with named entity recognition is meaning disambiguation (introduced by homonyms), which is being solved by approaches working with term contexts [31].

Apart from "document-driven" approaches that are used for annotating documents the "ontology-driven" approaches focus on populating the domain (or general) ontologies by expanding their hierarchical structure. An example of such approach is the *OntoSyphon* (created by McDowell and Cafarella), which has a purpose of finding instances (or subclasses) for a given ontology class [46]. Their approach, designed to work independently on domain it is used in, takes a domain ontology and text corpus (ultimately—the whole Web) as an input and outputs a ranked list of candidate instances for a class, also given on input. More detailed, the OntoSyphon works as follows:

1. The textual representation of the input class is retrieved from the ontology.
2. Textual phrases and sentences where the input class is used are retrieved from ontology (if present). Alternatively the ontology neighbors of the input class (parent classes, siblings in hierarchy, other related classes) are retrieved to form artificial phrases.
3. These phrases are used as queries for keyword search engine operating over the given document corpus (here, the whole Web can be easily used).
4. The search engine retrieves a set of documents to be mined. Because of the phrase use, only documents with proper term meanings are retrieved. Without the phrase search, i.e. with only a keyword search with textual representation of the input class, the system might encounter polysemy problems. If, for example, there was a class "sea", by querying it, we would retrieve documents about sea as a part of ocean, but also about SEA information system. But if the phrase is derived out of the existing ontology (e.g., "sea ship") and used as a query, much more coherent set of documents with a proper term meaning usage would be retrieved.
5. Finally, using the predefined set of sentence templates (e.g., "A is a B" or "A such as B, C, D"), the OntoSyphon matches the texts of the retrieved documents for expressions of the hierarchical subordination of the named entities, with input class being the superior entity. The other participating entities are afterward written to a instance candidate list.

2.4.2 Relationship Discovery and Naming

Another group of automated semantics acquisition approaches orients on the discovery relationships between entities. The entities can be anything from the simple terms to refined ontology concepts. In all cases, textual representations of entities are sought in the textual resources and subsequently their relationships are mined. The factual statements are often contained within the single sentence as subject, object (nouns, adjectives) and predicate (verbs), so many approaches focus on mining the sentences for term relationships [51, 60, 71]. Others try to exploit structures like tables and lists to access the relationship expressed through them [15].

An example of relationship harvesting was presented by Pantel and Pennacchiotti [51]. Their approach implemented a bootstrapping technique, which is, when supplied by few examples, able to harvest quality relationships from the natural language text corpus, even the whole Web. The approach is predicate-oriented: it primarily looks for relationship (predicate) occurrence in the corpus and only afterward, it attaches the subjects and objects to it. The method works as follows:

- At start-up a small set of seed expressions of the same relationship is chosen, e.g., "part of", "consists of", "comprises". Its generic pattern is created to cover variations of the expression, e.g., "X of Y".

- The bootstrapping technique relies on initial retrieval of large set of potential occurrences of the given seed patterns (which are a phrase stubs). The retrieval is done through a web search engine (or similar engine working over some other corpus).
- With a necessary preprocessing (trimming away the HTML, fragments of texts), the candidate sentences are prepared. Not all of them semantically match the start-up relationship, e.g., "wheel of the car" is correct while "house of representatives" is incorrect relation instance to "part of" relation.
- However, if a certain couple of subject-object (features) is recurring with different seeds, the features are arguably the in the given relationship (in this example, we have of course suppressed the algorithm of feature (entity) recognition).

Another and yet similar "predicate-oriented" approach was presented by Sanchez and Moreno [59, 60] who focused on exploration of non-taxonomic relationships which are insufficiently present in ontologies. It extracts domain-related verbs first and afterward tries to acquire their occurrences in the Web (access through search engine, using verb phrases learned from small domain-related corpus).

There is also an interesting work of Weichselbraun et al., which focuses on labeling (i.e. assigns types or names) of the already existing relationships (also stressing non-taxonomic relationships) [71]. The method mines the corpus of texts looking for co-occurrence of entities coupled in unlabeled relationship and looks up for candidate predicates. The process is, however, supervised by two ontologies: (1) which contains a predefined, finite set of possible relationship labels (domain-related), (2) which contains a taxonomy of all the entities involved in the unlabeled relationships. The purpose of the second ontology is to provide additional constraints that are defined on abstract layers of the ontology and thus have to be valid for lower levels too (which effectively means that not all verbs can be assigned as labels to certain relationships, even if they are found by text mining as candidates).

It is also necessary to mention lightweight semantics acquisition. Typically, latent semantic analysis is used as a "generalized vector space method that uses dimension reduction to generate term correlations" [53]. These correlations or co-occurrences of terms form a network of related terms, if we adopt the premise that if certain terms occurs together often, they are somehow semantically related (although we cannot name the relationship). But even such lightweight semantics are usable (e.g., for query expansion). Moreover unnamed relationships can always be processed by naming approaches and promoted to full triplets.

2.4.3 Automated Multimedia Description Acquisition

Despite their heterogeneous nature in terms of quality, automated metadata acquisition approaches are generally used for annotation of large resource collections. As first major group, we take the image description acquisition approaches.

Many approaches aim to identify semantics relevant to content of static images via identification of visual features. All of these approaches involve some degree of supervision. Duygulu and Barnard [22] employed segmentation of the image and associated identified features within individual segments with words from a large vocabulary. The vocabulary was used afterward to identify the semantics of the image. Their evaluation over Corel 5K dataset yielded 70 % correct prediction. Better results were achieved when a probabilistic model was employed by Lavrenko et al. [37].

Feng et al. [25] proposed enhancement to the segmentation approach, which employed the co-occurrence of terms related to images (e.g., tiger—grass occurring more frequently than tiger—building), which also improved output correctness but was more bound to the training data set of images. Improvements were also achieved when information about global and local features were used together [10].

Various approaches use machine learning for image or image region categorization. Techniques such as SVM [17] or Bayes point machine [16] perform well (precisions over 90 % in Corel 5K dataset), but are limited to a small number of categories and lack of training sets to be used effectively for acquisition of more specific metadata.

Due to its non-textual nature, metadata acquisition for image resources is often performed via analysis of their context (e.g., in the web environment) which may contain text or already annotated resources [52, 69, 70]. The acquisition of the semantics of multimedia content (visual or aural) may also involve OCR or speech recognition approaches [13].

Similarly to images, the raw audio resources are extensive and syntactically complex. Automated acquisition of their semantics is complicated. With images, we are usually satisfied with metadata telling us about physical features in them. The palette of metadata types is wider comprising not only track names, authors, publishers but also lyrics, melody, style, tonality, rhythm, motives or even mood the track evokes on listening. For music information retrieval, the latter group is just as important as the first group. They are used for "querying by example", which have proliferated next to the standard textual querying [42]. Music metadata are also much more abstract and a potential approach for their acquisition needs to perform sophisticated interpretations of the raw music track.

Many music metadata acquisition approaches involve as a first step a transformation of raw music stream to more symbolic representation, such as musical score or rhythm transcription. An approach of Lu and Hanjalic [41] identifies audio elements (natural semantic sound clusters, e.g., a sequence of chords). Authors point out the similarity of these elements to the words in texts (e.g., a sequence of tones can be understand as a sequence of characters). Thus, the music track can be mined for *keywords*, i.e. the most prominent audio elements. Still, these audio "keywords" cannot be used as normal textual keywords (for textual query formulation). Nevertheless, they provide a basis for effective music track comparison.

A different pre-processing technique was devised by Magistrali et al., who transformed the raw music tracks to an extensive XML and then RDF files. These were then interpreted by rules expertly prepared in an ontology and transformed to more symbolic representations (still in rdf) [42]. A more supervised, ontology-driven approach, than the "keyword" approach of Lu and Hanjalic, which reminds us of the unsupervised TF-IDF.

The preprocessed audio streams are subjected to further analysis, detecting more complex features and patterns of the music, eventually giving out the desired metadata about their aural characteristics. The unsupervised approaches produce unlabeled features (used mainly in example querying) using mostly statistical process modeling and machine learning [40, 50, 56]. There are also supervised, ontology-driven feature identification approaches [65]. Apart from content-based, also context-based approaches are used [26, 61].

2.5 Crowdsourcing

Crowdsourcing. The term itself was first coined in 2005 by Howe [29]. In 2008, Daren C. Brabham defined it as "an online, distributed problem-solving and production model". Crowdsourcing (and crowd-based approaches for semantics acquisition) emerged along with the Web 2.0 phenomenon, which enabled masses of Web users to be contributors of the Web content. The crowdsourcing often comprises *human computation* and is focused towards solving of the *human intelligence tasks*—tasks hard or impossible to be solved by computers, but relatively easy for humans. As Quinn and Bederson remind us, these two terms should not be confused [55]. While the "crowdsourcing" primarily designates the distribution of a task to the wide and open mass of people, the "human computation" designates the using of human power for solving of a problem with a computational nature (i.e. a problem that may be solved by computers at some point in the future).

The semantics acquisition involves many tasks performed via crowdsourcing. Users of the Web are time-to-time (and in various contexts) motivated to disclose some descriptive information about web resources they encounter. They comment and rate images or videos, manage their personal content applications, galleries and bookmarks. By collecting these information and tracking user behavior, crowdsourcing techniques produce resource descriptions and even lightweight domain models.

If the crowdsourced semantics originates from the human work, then what differences it have to expert approaches we mentioned earlier? The answer is the different quality assurance mechanisms. While manual approaches rely on an expertise of the individual, the crowd-based approaches the agreement principle: if many, even uninitiated people independently express the same fact, it is probably a truth (e.g., the same photo gets decorated with same tag from multiple users). This allows crowdsourcing to produce relatively precise outputs even if the input is noisy (an individual uninitiated user may produce many untrue suggestions).

The advantage of crowdsourcing approaches against the expert-based approaches is much greater scale of discovered semantics. First, the quantity of potential lay (non-expert) contributors is larger (even when they are used redundantly). On the other hand, experts are sometimes unavailable. Second, lay contributors are much cheaper or even free (resp. they are not paid for solving a task).

2.5.1 Crowdsourcing Classifications

In general, crowdsourcing comes in many different flavors. It also has very strong overlap with other terms such a human computation, social computing, collective intelligence, crowd computing. Together, they comprise a loosely bounded field and several researchers reflected the lack of abstract, formal models describing it. This resulted into several survey publications, attempting to conceptualize the field with variety of classifications [19, 21, 23, 54, 55].

In his position paper, Erickson classifies the crowdsourcing systems according to distribution of the crowd in time and space [23] (being either at the same time/place or not). This results into four categories of crowdsourcing:

- *Audience based*, when entire crowd participates at the same time and space.
- *Event based*, when the crowd is geographically distributed, but works at the same time on a common goal (e.g., innovation competition).
- *Geocentric*, when the work is done at a particular geographical location by multiple workers in different times (e.g., communal problem reporting).
- *Global*, when the process is bound neither to time nor space.

The typical Crowd-based semantics acquisition approaches (e.g., semantics acquisition games) are found in the latter category (global), as there is usually no need to bound them to specific time or place (though as a significant exception, various geocentric applications for collecting metadata on points of interest, e.g., FourSquare, should be mentioned).

Doan et al. defines nine dimensions according to which the crowdsourcing applications could be considered [21]. We look at six of these dimensions interesting through prism of crowd-based semantics acquisition:

- *What type of target problem is being solved (e.g., labeling images, building a knowledge base, rating movies)?*
- *What is the nature of collaboration?* Authors identify two major groups of approaches: *explicit* (where users explicitly collaborate to create an useful artifact as their primary objective) and *implicit* (where users solve a target problem as a side effect of another activity). The semantics acquisition tasks fall in both categories. The explicit approaches include item rating or knowledge base (ontology) building, the implicit comprise for example, image tagging through crowdsourcing games.
- *How does the application recruit and retain new workers?* This perspective brings up the question of incentives to the workers. Some semantics acquisition applications are useful for the user himself (e.g., tagging websites in bookmark portal), some rely on volunteers (e.g., contribution to knowledge bases like ConceptNet), some motivate by entertainment (e.g., crowdsourcing games).

- *What do users do in the process (how they solve the tasks)?* What technique is used by users to contribute (e.g., tagging, rating, reviewing)? How cognitively- or skill-demanding? Here, applications that ask simpler questions retrieve more answers from more workers but may also demand more validation (e.g., when workers validate existing metadata by dichotomic yes-no options). Is the semantics (being retrieved) a common sense knowledge or a specialized domain knowledge (which is obviously harder to obtain due to smaller pool of potential contributors)?
- *How are the partial results combined?* And how is the problem decomposed prior to that? In semantics acquisition, many approaches tend to collect atomic pieces of information (tags, triplets) which then (automatically) constitute more complex structures. A contrast to this are, for example, contributors to Wikipedia, that compose complex structures (texts) themselves and where the contribution combining is a demanding human intelligence task itself.
- *How is the output evaluated?* Common for semantics acquisition is redundant task solving and collaborative filtering—a technique possible mainly due to the "atomicity" of the acquired information. Apart from this, however, other techniques exist, such as rating of contributions created by other users, post hoc cleaning by domain experts or detection of suspicious behavior of workers (and thus, malicious contributions).

At approximately same time as Doan et al., Quinn and Bederson offered a different conceptualization and design space of the "combined" fields. Although they focused primarily on the human computation (rather than crowdsourcing) [55] and offered a classification of human computation approaches, their classification dimensions strongly refer to the crowdsourcing too. For each dimension, Quinn and Bederson also name several values, i.e. typical design patterns or features utilized by human computation systems. At the same time, they declare the list as open and waiting to be filled with new alternatives.

- *Motivation.* What motivates people to contribute? This dimension is directly mappable to Doan's "recruitment and retention". As major incentive forms, Quinn and Bederson identifies pay, reputation, altruism, enjoyment and "implicit" work (covered by Doan's "nature of collaboration").
- *Quality control.* Another "recurring" dimension of Doan's: "output evaluation". Though, Quinn and Bederson offer a finer-grained set of patterns. Many of them represent some kind of redundant task solving, common for semantics acquisition: output and input agreement (a reference to work of Luis von Ahn's semantics acquisition games [1]), redundancy, statistical filtering.
- *Aggregation.* Describes how are the individual worker contributions combined. A dimension directly mappable to Doan's "partial result combination". Authors identify a variety of approaches, including iterative improvement (or validation) of existing artifacts, searching for positive cases (e.g., visual scanning of large set of satellite images for evidence) or evaluation of fenotypes of genetic algorithms. More characteristic for semantics acquisition however, is simple collecting of partial contributions into a larger structure (e.g., atomic facts into an ontology),

feeding training data to machine learning approaches (e.g., training set of images with metadata) or using no aggregation at all.

- *Human skill.* What type of cognitive activity are the workers performing? Authors mention visual recognition, language understanding and human communication. The visual recognition together with aural recognition is often a case of multimedia metadata acquisition approaches. As another human skill category, we recognize the application of "common sense" which is a subject of several knowledge acquisition projects [39]. We see two counterparts to this dimension in Doan's work: the "target problem (type)" and "how do workers solve the task" (what tools or techniques they use). In both cases however, Doan et al. focus on "outer" characteristics of the job, whereas Quinn and Bederson focus on mind skills themselves. An attempt to categorize human skills used in human computation was also made later work by Parshotam [54], who identifies them as human perception (sensing), cognition, knowledge, common sense, visual processing, anomaly detection or context identification.
- *Process order.* For this dimension, authors identify three roles found in each human computation system: the requester, worker and computer. Then, several classes of systems based on order of work of these roles are presented. Sometimes, the computational task is firstly attempted by a computer and then corrected or complemented by a human, e.g., computer-worker-requester for ReCAPTCHA.[4] In other cases, the human contribution precedes the computer processing, e.g., a semantics acquisition game Peekaboom, where players identify visual objects by circular regions in the images which are further automatically folded to form true (i.e. noncircular) boundaries of these objects [2]. For semantics acquisition, both cases are common. Moreover, the role of computer processing (either prior or posterior), not only for mediation is often essential to handle the quantity of tasks (high even for a crowd processing).
- *Task-request cardinality.* How many workers are necessary to finish one task?

The authors encourage to further experimentation with the classification by combining various dimensions and their values to imagine new systems.

Based on the literature review, the (1) role of incentives (motivation) and (2) quality control receive most of the attention of researchers in crowdsourcing and human computation ([19, 57, 64] resp. [3, 19, 45, 73]).

2.5.2 Mechanical Turk

As a demonstration and a single most renown product (and at the same time, an approach) of the crowdsourcing the Wikipedia is often presented. A much more characteristic to the crowdsourcing principles however, is the *Amazon Mechanical Turk*.[5] It is a generic platform for controlled crowdsourcing, where companies or

---

[4] http://www.google.com/reCAPTCHA

[5] https://www.mturk.com

individuals (task owners) submit tasks they need to solve by a crowd (e.g., annotation of image collection). When the tasks are submitted the Turk organizes contributors to solve them, following the instructions given by task owner (e.g., how many times a particular task instance should be solved, what criteria a contributor must fulfill).

A significant feature of the Mechanical Turk are micro payments to contributors (usually units of cents) for each task solved. Micro payments represent important motivation for contributors to participate in the process. It is sometimes secondary to other, primary motivation, but is necessary. A good example of this is participation in a crowd-based scientific experiment evaluation (e.g., validation of resource metadata): the contributor is sympathetic to the cause, but the definitive incentive to join the process is the money (although small) he receives for the job [58].

Apart from this model, there are also crowdsourcing approaches that employ contributors *without* the need of motivating them by monetary values. Almost exclusively, the semantics are then only a side-product of the user activity, which primarily focused on their needs (e.g., social bookmarks, comments). Sometimes, users do not even know they are contributing to some knowledge base. Due to these facts, possible kinds of semantics we can collect via crowdsourcing is limited with types of activities the users usually do on the Web (although there is always a possibility to attract their attention to some new activity). For example, common users of the Web upload and annotate (textually with tags) images. They do this, because they want to have them organized, always available and shareable to friends (e.g., Flickr[6] image gallery), not because they should be annotated. In social networks like *Facebook*, users locate exact position of persons in the images. However, we can hardly expect them being motivated to locate non-living things (which also deserve such annotations).

2.5.3 Delicious

A typical case of semantics acquisition via crowdsourcing is the bookmarking portal Delicious.[7] Here, users submit URLs they want to visit later or simply have them at hand for some reason, similarly to web browser bookmarks. Here, however, they have them online so they do not have to create them repeatedly on different workstations and moreover, they decorate them with tags (the submission procedure requests the user to provide some tags). Using the tags, the URLs can be easily filtered and even large set of bookmarks are relatively easy to browse (e.g., by using tag clouds).

From the Semantic Web perspective, the Delicious users do two useful things:

1. They **decorate URLs**, i.e. web resources, *with tags* and annotate them. Unfortunately, they do it with respect to themselves, i.e. they write tags which meaning they understand, but this meaning can be proprietary to them only and therefore confusing or inaccurate for the rest of the world. For example, someone bookmarks the Wikipedia page about grizzly but decorates it with tag "55 km/hr",

---

[6] http://www.flickr.com

[7] http://delicious.org

which for the user represents the speed of the bear and makes perfect sense since he is collecting articles to create ranking of animal speed. But from the universal point of view, this tag represents only a marginal part of the article. Another drawback of user tagging is the relative generality of the used words (causing overload of the tags lowering their distinctive ability) and often use of sentiment or even irony with no semantic feedback on the content of the URL-identified resources (e.g., "funny", "gorgeous", "stunning") [49].

2. **Generate tag collocations**. When a user decorates a resource with more than one tag, he expresses the, yet unspecified, relatedness of these tags. These collocations are afterward used to create a lightweight tag folksonomy [49].

Even with all drawbacks, the user tagging is a potent source of lightweight semantics and annotations. Using the agreement principle and dictionary, more clean metadata can be obtained and utilized like, for instance, in the project *Treelicious* which combines the delicious folksonomy with *WordNet* hierarchy to create a navigable tag structure.

The associations between term relationships in folksonomies like delicious are unknown, meaning that we do not know, what does the relationship means. Some researchers build upon the folksonomies like Delicious and leverage their term relationships by identifying their specific types. In their work, Barla and Bieliková [7] extract hierarchical relationship between terms with syntactical analysis of the term graph structure.

2.5.4 Wikipedia and DBpedia

The DBpedia is an example of semantic building approach that mixes all manual, crowdsourcing and automated approaches. It is closely related to world largest and collaboratively created encyclopedia, the Wikipedia. Although the Wikipedia's articles can be seen as being created manually by pseudo-experts, the large number and the collaboration of the contributors pushes it rather to the crowdsourcing category of knowledge acquisition. While Wikipedia is primarily made readable to human users, the DBpedia transcripts the knowledge contained in Wikipedia to a more "machine-friendly" ontology, using RDF and OWL standards.

The basis of the DBpedia content is created automatically: Each article of Wikipedia becomes a concept in DBpedia. Using various algorithms, the texts and links of Wikipedia are mined to create relationships and assign properties to the concepts. These include [12]:

- Extraction of labels from titles and link named entities.
- Abstract extraction from original article texts.
- Article categories.
- Geo-coordinates.
- Properties through infoboxes. Infoboxes are structured information attached to some articles, consisting of properties and their values. The infoboxes of articles

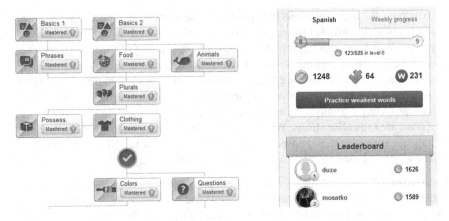

Fig. 2.1 Example of various Duolingo achievements, constantly reminding student of his progress and inviting for more activity

of same category follow the same structure, so it is relevant to use their properties as attributes of the category (a superclass) in the DBpedia (e.g., articles about kings of France are decorated with reign time span and prime minister attributes).

The DBpedia also pays respect to other existing global (semantic) data resources (like FOAF ontology). Unfortunately the automatically extracted facts of DBpedia are still somewhat sparse. Although the ontology contains a solid concept hierarchy, which originates from the manually created and refined Wikipedia classification system, it lacks relevant non-taxonomic relationships (e.g., composition, interaction).

2.5.5 Duolingo: A "Gamified" Crowdsourcing

One of the incentives used to motivate workers to participate in a crowdsourcing process is the gamification: an introduction of game elements (e.g., leaderboards, badges, achievements) into activities that are not games themselves. By its definition, gamification covers any working activity (not just crowdsourcing), with crowdsourcing however, it is with good symbiosis: the small tasks allow fluent rise of player's "achievement" levels, constantly reminding of his progress. A good example of fusing gamification and crowdsourcing is a language learning portal called Duolingo[8] created by Luis von Ahn. In Duolingo, a student may learn a new language from scratch, using interactive exercises that automatically evaluate his written or even spoken answers. For this, student receives various achievements and badges (see Fig. 2.1)—he is constantly reminded of his progress.

---

[8] https://www.duolingo.com

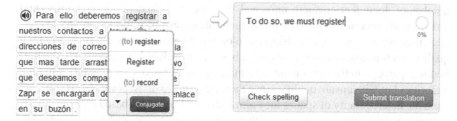

Fig. 2.2 Example of Duolingo's interface for translating real Web. The application aid the student with translation of individual work, making him practice with vocabulary and able to translate even complex sentences

But Duolingo has also its crowdsourcing part: as a practice, its students can translate real sentences from web pages written in the foreign language to English. For this, a convenient interface (see Fig. 2.2) is provided. The student may also review and rate other translations. For these activities, he is also rewarded with achievement points. Using a redundancy principle and a wisdom of the crowd, Duolingo is able to output very accurate translations of a real web pages using only a group of lay translators that are actually *just learning* the language.

2.5.6 Crowdsourcing Games

The gamification aims to solve the problem of limited motivation to participate in a crowdsourcing by using game-like elements. As such, it may be perceived as a springboard towards "full" *crowdsourcing games*—a part of the crowdsourcing approach family. These games emerged as an alternative to solving computational problems, hard or impossible to be solved by machine computation (which includes acquiring semantic structures), via aggregation of knowledge provided by many non-expert users (e.g., for image annotation) [62]. Crowdsourcing games transform problems into games that motivate players to solve them via fun and thus eliminate the need to pay them. As many game instances can be played simultaneously, they are suitable for larger scale problems divisible into smaller tasks. Compared to other crowdsourcing techniques, the knowledge gained in crowdsourcing games is not just a by-product of another user activity (e.g., annotating web resources for personal use), but the *primary* objective, so their design is tuned to maximize that ability. The crowdsourcing games are discussed in detail in the Chap. 3.

2.6 Discussion

To sum up, there is a variety of approaches for building web semantics ranging from manual through crowdsourcing to automated ones. Semantics discovery approaches are evaluated with respect to quantity (number of instances retrieved, number of document covered, universal versus domain specific applicability) and quality (tolerance to bias and errors, structural degree) of information and knowledge they are able to acquire. Using these perspectives, we observe a generally high quality and low quantity results of expert based approaches that are bound to the limited manpower. On the other hand, automated approaches deliver semantics in high quantities but with unsure quality, since they are prone to unusual situations sourcing from the heterogeneity of spaces they aim to cover. The crowd-based approaches are somewhere in between, operating with numerous, yet lay mass of human contributors. They have potential for both quality and quantity, but are limited by specificness of the task they aim to fulfill. They also need to motivate the contributors the right way, which is also limiting. These (but not only these) issues make the field of crowdsourcing a target for researchers.

Some researchers argue there is no other way to create accurate domain models and annotations, than to utilize manpower, others argue that virtually any piece of knowledge is already on the Web, probably with great redundancy and it is only a matter of developing of the ultimate harvesting algorithm to collect it [18].

For now, the best way toward acquisition of semantics lie in combining approach families together to exploit strong points and neutralize weaknesses. As an example of approach chaining, we can imagine a ontology engineering project where experts firstly set top layers of the taxonomy within the ontology, set up the axioms and entity and relationship types and seed the examples. After this, an automated method is deployed over the corresponding text resource corpus and extracts entities and relationships according to patterns (previously set by expert). Lastly, the crowd comes in to validate the acquired entities and relationships using a simple true/false question answering interface. As another example of symbiosis, we can consider a crowd that prepares image tags for images prior to the automated classifier training.

Considering this, we come to two possible roles of the crowd: semantics creation or semantics validation. Whether the crowd is supposed to carry out first or the latter, greatly influences the options the method designer has. Naturally, a "validation" crowdsourcing always depends on an existing metadata set it aims to improve. On the other hand it has a great advantage regarding the design of the contributor's interface with the crowdsourcing platform: validating something is in general more ergonomic than creating (both syntactically and semantically). In the context of the first example, a dichotomous question answering about the validity of a typed relationship between two terms is syntactically easier than selecting the type from a long list. This somewhat advocates the use of crowdsourcing for semantic validation rather creation, especially if the automated method that creates the metadata is able to state its confidence (support) about its output, limiting the metadata set that needs to be validated to only "unsure" cases.

The type of the resource for which the semantics is created also indicates the potential outcome of the acquisition method. For structured and unstructured texts, automated approaches function better if only lightweight structures are demanded (e.g., keywords), whereas experts or crowds are needed, if the semantics (especially domain models) is required on a higher quality grade. With multimedia, the human work is even more demanded in semantics creation. For our research presented in this book, we identified a particular domain of personal image metadata creation, in which all families of approaches are nowadays shorthanded. The personal multimedia creation cannot be subjected to either automated means or crowds, because neither of these possesses the specific knowledge (e.g., awareness about person names or specific places).

As another issue, we address in this book, we identified the upkeep of the semantics. Nowadays, researchers are primarily focused on semantics creation and only little attention is given to already created semantics. Yet, this existing corpora must be constantly reviewed, validated and updated. Many times, metadata are temporal "by definition" or are invalidated by the change of the underlying resource. The metadata may also be wrong from the moment they are created (after all, the automated and crowd-based method are sometimes prone to errors). All of these "effects" may render a metadata corpus partially invalid and a needed subject to cleanup (removing incorrect or invalid facts) and a potential "renovation" of semantics (creating new, correct facts to as substitute the removed). In this work, we chose the domain of music metadata corpora, created by human taggers, as a candidate for metadata cleanup (realized through crowdsourcing games).

References

1. von Ahn, L., Dabbish, L.: Designing games with a purpose. Commun. ACM 51(8), 58–67 (2008)
2. von Ahn, L., Liu, R., Blum, M.: Peekaboom: a game for locating objects in images. In: Proceedings of the SIGCHI Conference on Human Factors in Computing Systems, CHI '06, pp. 55–64. ACM, New York (2006) NULL
3. Baba, Y., Kashima, H.: Statistical quality estimation for general crowdsourcing tasks. In: Proceedings of the 19th ACM SIGKDD International Conference on Knowledge Discovery and Data Mining. KDD '13, pp. 554–562. ACM, New York (2013)
4. Bai, J., Song, D., Bruza, P., Nie, J.Y., Cao, G.: Query expansion using term relationships in language models for information retrieval. In: Proceedings of the 14th ACM International Conference on Information and Knowledge Management, CIKM '05, pp. 688–695. ACM, New York (2005)
5. Barathi, M.: Context disambiguation based semantic web search for effective information retrieval. J. Comput. Sci. 7(4), 548–553 (2011)
6. Barla, M.: Towards social-based user modeling and personalization. Inf. Sci. Technol. Bull. ACM Slovakia 3(1), 52–60 (2011)
7. Barla, M., Bieliková, M.: On deriving tagsonomies: keyword relations coming from crowd. In: Proceedings of the 1st International Conference on Computational Collective Intelligence, Semantic Web, Social Networks and Multiagent Systems, ICCCI '09, pp. 309–320. Springer, Berlin, Heidelberg (2009)
8. Barla, M., Bieliková, M., Ezzeddinne, A.B., Kramár, T., Šimko, M., Vozár, O.: On the impact of adaptive test question selection for learning efficiency. Comput. Educ. 55(2), 846–857 (2010)
9. Bhogal, J., Macfarlane, A., Smith, P.: A review of ontology based query expansion. Inf. Process. Manage. 43(4), 866–886 (2007)
10. Bieliková, M., Kuric, E.: Automatic image annotation using global and local features. In: Proceedings of the 2011 Sixth International Workshop on Semantic Media Adaptation and Personalization. SMAP '11, pp. 33–38. IEEE Computer Society, Washington (2011)

11. Bizer, C., Heath, T., Berners-Lee, T.: Linked data—the story so far. Int. J. Semant. Web Inf. Syst. **5**(3), 1–22 (2009)
12. Bizer, C., Lehmann, J., Kobilarov, G., Auer, S., Becker, C., Cyganiak, R., Hellmann, S.: Dbpedia—a crystallization point for the web of data. Web Semant. **7**, 154–165 (2009)
13. Bolettieri, P., Falchi, F., Gennaro, C., Rabitti, F.: Automatic metadata extraction and indexing for reusing e-learning multimedia objects. In: Workshop on Multimedia Information Retrieval on The Many Faces of Multimedia Semantics. MS '07, pp. 21–28. ACM, New York (2007)
14. Botev, C., Amer-Yahia, S., Shanmugasundaram, J.: Expressiveness and performance of full-text search languages. In: Proceedings of the 10th International Conference on Advances in Database Technology. EDBT'06, pp. 349–367. Springer, Berlin, Heidelberg (2006)
15. Buitelaar, P., Cimiano, P., Frank, A., Hartung, M., Racioppa, S.: Ontology-based information extraction and integration from heterogeneous data sources. Int. J. Hum Comput Stud. **66**(11), 759–788 (2008)
16. Chang, E., Goh, K., Sychay, G., Wu, G.: Cbsa: content-based soft annotation for multimodal image retrieval using bayes point machines. IEEE Trans. Cir. and Sys. Video Technol. **13**(1), 26–38 (2003)
17. Cusano, C., Ciocca, G., Schettini, R.: Image annotation using SVM. Proc. SPIE **5304**, 330–338 (2004)
18. Dalvi, N., Kumar, R., Pang, B., Ramakrishnan, R., Tomkins, A., Bohannon, P., Keerthi, S., Merugu, S.: A web of concepts. In: Proceedings of the Twenty-Eighth ACM SIGMOD-SIGACT-SIGART Symposium on Principles of Database Systems, pp. 1–12. ACM (2009)
19. Das, R., Vukovic, M.: Emerging theories and models of human computation systems: a brief survey. In: Proceedings of the 2nd International Workshop on Ubiquitous Crowdsouring, Ubi-Crowd '11, pp. 1–4. ACM, New York (2011)
20. Di Maio, P.: 'Just enough' ontology engineering. In: Proceedings of the International Conference on Web Intelligence, Mining and Semantics, WIMS '11, pp. 8:1–8:10. ACM, New York (2011)
21. Doan, A., Ramakrishnan, R., Halevy, A.Y.: Crowdsourcing systems on the world-wide web. Commun. ACM **54**(4), 86–96 (2011)
22. Duygulu, P., Barnard, K.: Freitas, J.F.G.d., Forsyth, D.A.: Object recognition as machine translation: Learning a lexicon for a fixed image vocabulary. In: Proceedings of the 7th European Conference on Computer Vision-Part IV. ECCV '02, pp. 97–112. Springer, London (2002)
23. Erickson, T.: Some thoughts on a framework for crowdsourcing. In: Proceedings of the SIGCHI Conference on Human Factors in Computing Systems, CHI'11. A Position Paper for the CHI 2011 Workshop on Crowdsourcing and Human Computation. ACM, New York (2011)
24. Fellbaum, C. (ed.): WordNet: An Electronic Lexical Database. MIT Press, Cambridge, MA (1998)
25. Feng, S.L., Manmatha, R., Lavrenko, V.: Multiple bernoulli relevance models for image and video annotation. In: Proceedings of the 2004 IEEE Computer Society Conference on Computer Vision and Pattern Recognition. CVPR'04, pp. 1002–1009. IEEE Computer Society, Washington (2004)
26. Ferrara, A., Ludovico, L.A., Montanelli, S., Castano, S., Haus, G.: A semantic web ontology for context-based classification and retrieval of music resources. ACM Trans. Multimedia Comput. Commun. Appl. **2**(3), 177–198 (2006)
27. Guarino, N., Welty, C.: Evaluating ontological decisions with ontoclean. Commun. ACM **45**(2), 61–65 (2002)
28. Gulla, J.A., Sugumaran, V.: An interactive ontology learning workbench for non-experts. In: Proceedings of the 2nd International Workshop on Ontologies and Information Systems for the Semantic Web. ONISW '08, pp. 9–16. ACM, New York (2008)
29. Howe, J.: The rise of crowdsourcing. Wired Mag. **14**(6) (2006). http://www.wired.com/wired/archive/14.06/crowds.html
30. Jarrar, M.: Position paper: towards the notion of gloss, and the adoption of linguistic resources in formal ontology engineering. In: Proceedings of the 15th International Conference on World Wide Web. WWW '06, pp. 497–503. ACM, New York (2006)

31. Jačala, M., Tvarožek, J.: Named entity disambiguation based on explicit semantics. In: Proceedings of the 38th International Conference on Current Trends in Theory and Practice of Computer Science, SOFSEM'12, pp. 456–466. Springer, Berlin, Heidelberg (2012)

32. Kalfoglou, Y., Schorlemmer, M.: Ontology mapping: the state of the art. Knowl. Eng. Rev. 18(1):1–31 (2003)

33. Köhler, J., Philippi, S., Specht, M., Rüegg, A.: Ontology based text indexing and querying for the semantic web. Know. Based Syst. 19(8), 744–754 (2006)

34. Kompan, M., Zeleník, D., Bieliková, M.: Methods for personalized recommendation of newspaper articles. In: Znalosti (In Slovak) (2011)

35. Kozareva, Z.: Bootstrapping named entity recognition with automatically generated gazetteer lists. In: Proceedings of the Eleventh Conference of the European Chapter of the Association for Computational Linguistics: Student Research W. on - EACL '06, pp. 15–21. Association for Computational Linguistics, Morristown (2006)

36. Kramár, T., Barla, M., Bieliková, M.: Disambiguating search by leveraging the social network context based on the stream of user's activity. In: Proceedings of the 18th International Conference on User Modeling, Adaptation, and Personalization,UMAP '10, pp. 387–392. Springer, Hawaii (2010)

37. Lavrenko, V., Manmatha, R., Jeon, J.: A model for learning the semantics of pictures. In: Proceedings of Neural Information Processing Systems (NIPS). MIT Press, Cambridge (2003)

38. Lenat, D.B.: CYC: a large-scale investment in knowledge infrastructure. Commun. ACM 38(11), 33–38 (1995)

39. Liu, H., Singh, P.: Conceptnet—a practical commonsense reasoning tool-kit. BT Technol. J. 22(4), 211–226 (2004)

40. Liu, Q., Sung, A.H., Qiao, M.: Novel stream mining for audio steganalysis. In: Proceedings of the 17th ACM International Conference on Multimedia. MM '09, pp. 95–104. ACM, New York (2009)

41. Lu, L., Hanjalic, A.: Towards optimal audio "keywords" detection for audio content analysis and discovery. In: Proceedings of the 14th Annual ACM International Conference on Multimedia. MULTIMEDIA '06, pp. 825–834. ACM, New York (2006)

42. Magistrali, M., Catenazzi, N., Sommaruga, L.: Tonal mir: a music retrieval engine based on semantic web technologies. In: Proceedings of the 6th International Conference on Semantic Systems, I-SEMANTICS '10, pp. 21:1–21:5. ACM, New York (2010).

43. Maleewong, K., Anutariya, C., Wuwongse, V.: A semantic argumentation approach to collaborative ontology engineering. In: Proceedings of the 11th International Conference on Information Integration and Web-based Applications and Services. iiWAS '09, pp. 56–63. ACM, New York (2009)

44. Marchionini, G.: From finding to understanding. Commun. ACM 49(4), 41–46 (2006)

45. Mashhadi, A.J., Capra, L.: Quality control for real-time ubiquitous crowdsourcing. In: Proceedings of the 2nd International Workshop on Ubiquitous Crowdsouring. UbiCrowd '11, pp. 5–8. ACM, New York (2011)

46. Mcdowell, L., Cafarella, M.: Ontology-driven, unsupervised instance population. Web Semant. Sci. Serv. Agents World Wide Web 6(3), 218–236 (2008)

47. Mizoguchi, R., Sunagawa, E., Kozaki, K., Kitamura, Y.: The model of roles within an ontology development tool: Hozo. Appl. Ontol. 2(2), 159–179 (2007)

48. Moor, A.D., Leenheer, P.D., Meersman, R., Starlab, V.: Dogma-mess: a meaning evolution support system for interorganizational ontology engineering. In: Proceedings of the 14th International Conference on Conceptual Structures, (ICCS 2006), pp. 189–203. Springer, Heidelberg (2006)

49. Mullins, M., Fizzano, P.: Treelicious: a system for semantically navigating tagged web pages. IEEE/WIC/ACM International Conference on Web Intelligence and Intelligent Agent Technology, 3, 91–96 (2010)

50. Orio, N.: Automatic identification of audio recordings based on statistical modeling. Signal Process. 90(4), 1064–1076 (2010)

51. Pantel, P., Pennacchiotti, M.: Automatically harvesting and ontologizing semantic relations. In: Proceedings of the 2008 Conference on Ontology Learning and Population: Bridging the Gap between Text and Knowledge, pp. 171–195. IOS Press,Amsterdam (2008)

52. Papadopoulos, G.T., Mylonas, P., Mezaris, V., Avrithis, Y.S., Kompatsiaris, I.: Knowledge-assisted image analysis based on context and spatial optimization. Int. J. Semantic Web Inf. Syst. 2(3), 17–36 (2006)

53. Park, L.a.F., Ramamohanarao, K.: An analysis of latent semantic term self-correlation. ACM Trans. Inf. Syst. 27(2), 1–35 (2009)

54. Parshotam, K.: Crowd computing: a literature review and definition. In: Proceedings of the South African Institute for Computer Scientists and Information Technologists Conference. SAICSIT '13, pp. 121–130. ACM, New York (2013)

55. Quinn, A.J., Bederson, B.B.: Human computation: a survey and taxonomy of a growing field. In: Proceedings of the SIGCHI Conference on Human Factors in Computing Systems. CHI '11, pp. 1403–1412. ACM, New York (2011)

56. Radhakrishnan, R., Divakaran, A., Xiong, Z.: A time series clustering based framework for multimedia mining and summarization using audio features. In: Proceedings of the 6th ACM SIGMM International Workshop on Multimedia Information Retrieval. MIR '04, pp. 157–164. ACM, New York (2004)

57. Richter, S., Perkmann Berger, S., Koch, G., Füller, J.: Online idea contests: identifying factors for user retention. Proceedings of the 5th International Conference on Online Communities and Social Computing. OCSC'13, pp. 76–85. Springer, Berlin, Heidelberg (2013)

58. Sabou, M., Bontcheva, K., Scharl, A.: Crowdsourcing research opportunities: lessons from natural language processing. In: Proceedings of the 12th International Conference on Knowledge Management and Knowledge Technologies, i-KNOW '12, pp. 17:1–17:8. ACM, New York (2012)

59. Sanchez, D.: A methodology to learn ontological attributes from the web. Data Knowl. Eng. 69(6), 573–597 (2010)

60. Sanchez, D., Moreno, A.: Learning non-taxonomic relationships from web documents for domain ontology construction. Data Knowl. Eng. 64(3), 600–623 (2008)

61. Schedl, M., Widmer, G., Knees, P., Pohle, T.: A music information system automatically generated via web content mining techniques. Inf. Process. Manage. 47(3), 426–439 (2011)

62. Siorpaes, K., Hepp, M.: Games with a purpose for the semantic web. IEEE Intell. Syst. 23, 50–60 (2008)

63. Stewart, R., Scott, G., Zelevinsky, V.: Idea navigation: structured browsing for unstructured text. In: Proceeding of the Twenty-Sixth Annual SIGCHI Conference on Human Factors in Computing Systems, CHI '08, pp. 1789–1792. ACM, New York (2008)

64. Tokarchuk, O., Cuel, R., Zamarian, M.: Analyzing crowd labor and designing incentives for humans in the loop. IEEE Internet Comput. 16(5), 45–51 (2012)

65. Tsinaraki, C., Polydoros, P., Kazasis, F., Christodoulakis, S.: Ontology-based semantic indexing for mpeg-7 and tv-anytime audiovisual content. Multimedia Tools Appl. 26(3), 299–325 (2005)

66. Tudorache, T., Noy, N.F., Falconer, S.M., Musen, M.A.: A knowledge base driven user interface for collaborative ontology development. Proceedings of the 16th International Conference on Intelligent User Interfaces. IUI '11, pp. 411–414. ACM, New York (2011)

67. Tvarožek, M.: Exploratory search in the adaptive social semantic web. Inf. Sci. Technol. Bull. ACM Slovakia 3(1), 42–51 (2011)

68. Tvarožek, M., Bieliková, M.: Generating exploratory search interfaces for the semantic web. In:Forbrig, P., Paternó, F., Mark Pejtersen, A. (eds.) Human-Computer Interaction, IFIP Advances in Information and Communication Technology, vol. 332, pp. 175–186. Springer, Boston (2010)

69. Verborgh, R., Van Deursen, D., Mannens, E., Poppe, C., Van de Walle, R.: Enabling context-aware multimedia annotation by a novel generic semantic problem-solving platform. Multimedia Tools Appl. 61(1), 105–129 (2012)

70. Wang, Y., Mei, T., Gong, S., Hua, X.S.: Combining global, regional and contextual features for automatic image annotation. Pattern Recogn. 42(2), 259–266 (2009)

71. Weichselbraun, A., Wohlgenannt, G., Scharl, A.: Refining non-taxonomic relation labels with external structured data to support ontology learning. Data Knowl. Eng. **69**(8), 763–778 (2010)
72. Witbrock, M., Matuszek, C., Brusseau, A., Kahlert, R., Fraser, C.B., Lenat, D.: Knowledge begets knowledge: steps towards assisted knowledge acquisition in cyc. In: Proceedings of the AAAI (2005)
73. Zhu, S., Kane, S., Feng, J., Sears, A.: A crowdsourcing quality control model for tasks distributed in parallel. In: CHI '12 Extended Abstracts on Human Factors in Computing Systems. CHI EA '12, pp. 2501–2506. ACM, New York (2012)

Chapter 3
State-of-the-Art: Semantics Acquisition Games

Abstract In this chapter, we review the state-of-the-art of semantics acquisition games (SAGs), focusing primarily on the purposes these games fulfill. We first define the terms: crowdsourcing game, human-computation game, semantics acquisition game, serious game and game with a purpose. Then, we present a classification of semantics acquisition games' purposes, which nowadays range from multimedia metadata acquisition, through text annotation, building common knowledge bases to ontology creation and upkeep. For each category, we list and describe some of the typical games. We conclude the chapter with discussion on current limitations of SAGs, namely for the specific domains.

A *human computation game* is a computer game application, which, in addition to providing entertainment to its player, exploits the power of the human mind to solve a computational task that is hard or impossible to be solved by a computer, but easy to be solved by a human (a human intelligence task, HIT). This is done by special design of the game rules which force player to solve a problem or to disclose some of his knowledge. The idea of human computation game is based on the premise that though humans relax and have fun while playing, they meanwhile do non-trivial reasoning and problem solving during the game. This means a lot of "human cycles" performed during games may be harnessed to solve real problems.

When a human computation game engages a crowd of players for solving a task, we call it a *crowdsourcing game*. To this day, almost all of the human computation games are crowdsourcing games. Some games may be considered as exceptions, for example when they serve the individual players separately, rather than the owner of the game [17], but practically, these terms are interchangeable. The crowd of players is non-expert (regarding the task) and usually open. The crowdsourcing games typically use the redundant task solving and player agreement principle for their output validation. The main distinction of the crowdsourcing games within the crowdsourcing field is the motivation for participation in the process: the entertainment.

Finally, if the purpose of the game relates to creation or upkeep of semantics, we call the game a *semantics acquisition game* (SAG). For this book, this category is of the primary interest.

J. Šimko and M. Bieliková, *Semantic Acquisition Games*,
DOI: 10.1007/978-3-319-06115-3_3,
© Springer International Publishing Switzerland 2014

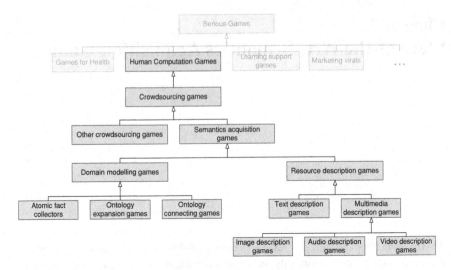

Fig. 3.1 A taxonomy of crowdsourcing games within serious games

As an illustrative example, the probably most successful SAG to this day, the ESP Game is often presented. The game acquires image descriptions (tags). It is a game for two players who are given the same image as only connection between them—they do not know each other and cannot communicate. Their task is to agree on the same word describing the given image and only after that they receive winning points. It is apparent that these players have virtually no chance of agreeing on a word that is not related to the image. Therefore if they agree on some, it is highly probable that this word describes the image and a textual annotation for the image can be created [24].

Naturally, crowdsourcing games are also a part of a group of computer programs we usually call *games* (with all their usual characteristics [16]). Between the two concepts ("the crowdsourcing game" and "the game"), in the concept hierarchy, lies the concept of *serious games*, which comprises all types of computer games, designed not only to entertain. These include marketing games, games for health or educational games [4]. The crowdsourcing games are just another category of serious games (the taxonomic overview of these concepts can be seen in the Fig. 3.1).

There is also another term for describing the crowdsourcing games (resp. semantics acquisition games)—the *game with a purpose* (GWAP). It was coined by Luis von Ahn [22] as a first term to describe this phenomenon and is often used in the literature. Yet, the use of the term is often disputed. At one point is used to describe the crowdsourcing games (or even semantics acquisition games only). On the other hand, if taken literally, the expression "with a purpose" may refer to any "useful" effect (apart from the entertainment) achieved by the game, so from that perspective it will fit to any "serious game". We therefore try not to use the term GWAP in this work, but but use "crowdsourcing game" and "semantics acquisition game" instead (unless we specifically refer to the works of Luis von Ahn).

As a related term to serious games, the term *gamification* [6], should also be mentioned. It represents a process of inserting game-like features like system of game-token rewarding or point competition into existing working schemes to increase the motivation of workers (e.g., for each completed task, an employee of a company receives virtual points or badges to compete with colleagues). The term is often misused for "serious game" because both concepts are meant to make "a work-like activity" a more pleasurable (entertaining, game-like) experience. However, the "gamifying" of a workflow does not make it a "game". On the other hand, the concept of gamification is often present in non-game crowdsourcing processes [23].

The gamification truly is what it sounds—an introduction of game elements (e.g. leaderboards, badges, achievements) into activities that are not games themselves. Its aim is to motivate workers to perform more. It is not an universal solution, it only works in specific circumstances (it must be meaningful for the workers to perform the task without game, it must look unique, impose challenges and promote worker skill). The gamification may only improve existing working process—it cannot "trick" workers doing a task they would not normally do. Despite these disadvantages it is a today's trend and is pursued by many companies.

There is hypothetically no limit on domain or type of a problem the crowdsourcing games can solve. Just to mention some, which are not related to semantics acquisition:

- **Plummings**—a game for optimization of FPGA circuits, a known NP-hard problem (i.e. hard to solve by a machine) [19]. In this game, the player acts as an architect and administrator of an artificial city inhabited by characters called *Plummings*. The Plummings live in special habitats that need to be effectively supplied with life-keeping substances. The player solves the logistical problems imposed by the structure of the city: the layout of habitats and supply lines, which he tries to optimize so his citizens can live. This covers the game story presented to player. In fact however, the storyline is just a facade. As the "background" of the game elements lie the real FPGA circuit components and their connections which must be optimized.
- **FoldIt**—a game for protein layout optimization [3]. In this game, the player manipulates the layout of virtual molecule models. His task is to layout a molecule so it fits a certain condition (e.g. to become an effective catalyst in certain reaction). The molecule has also be stable according to known chemical rules. For complex molecules this task cannot be automated. Starting with easy samples, the player gradually becomes capable of designing complex molecules and ultimately, some useful[1] ones.

Despite of these examples, crowdsourcing games are predominantly utilized for creation of semantics [15] (Fig. 3.1): resource description (of texts and multimedia) and domain modeling (entity identification, relationship discovery and naming). The

---

[1] Recently, the players of the FoldIt game have helped in discovering a protein with significant impact in cancer research.

probable reason for this is that metadata creation comprises mostly working with text and textual games are easy to create: most of the existing SAGs do not comprise elaborate graphics or 3D modeling as is common in most of today's games.

3.1 Image Description Games

First, we look at SAGs for multimedia metadata acquisition, in particular at image description SAGs. Image description is a task that humans can do much more effectively than machines, even today, when much work has been done in the field of automated image classification [10]. Generally, the image description is done by two steps: (1) symbolic interpretation of the (sub-symbolic) image bitmap (this is easily done by human brain with almost no effort) and (2) transcription of the symbols to the textual form. The latter is the step, which humans are not normally motivated to do, so SAGs focus on that part.

The already mentioned ESP Game [24] produces textual annotations in form of tags to images given as game input. This online game is played by two players (coupled randomly from the large pool of players) at the same time. The players are anonymous to each other, they cannot communicate. Both of them are shown the same image (as the one seen in the Fig. 3.2). Their task is to type in some words, describing the given image. When they have both typed the same word, they "win" the round.

The deployment of the ESP resulted in a massive collection of new metadata to images (partially because the game was adopted by Google company, which advertised it and used its results). The collected metadata also had a surprisingly good quality, which, in the end, had a significant impact on proliferation of the whole SAGs research field.

Motivated by several dishonest player behavior issues of the ESP game, a modification of its principle was made by Ho et al. in the game named *KissKissBan* [8]. It introduces a third player, *blocker*, as opponent to the first two players (couple). His task is to write tags relevant to the image earlier than the remaining players preventing them to use them for reaching agreement. According to authors, this modification brought two benefits: (1) third player effectively supervised any attempts of cheating by partner couple, (2) more specific and richer set of tags was used to describe images (since the obvious tags have been quickly banned). The authors evaluated the game in experiments (with 500 games) showing the increase in diversity of the acquired labels.

The SAGs (described above) focus on retrieval of proper tags describing the images. Luis von Ahn, however, went further toward identification of exact bitmap areas which objects occupy in the image. He designed the game *Peekaboom* [24], which uses the already tagged images from ESP Game and outputs contours of objects mentioned in the description tags.

Peekaboom is played by two players with two roles: *peek* and *boom* which are again two anonymous players, capable of communication only through the game

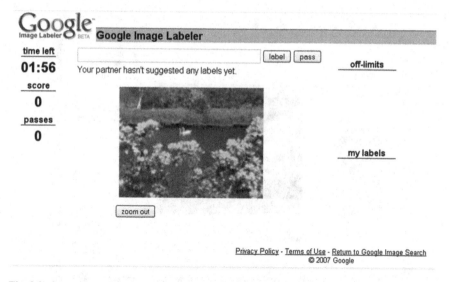

Fig. 3.2 Screenshot of the *google image labeler* implementation of the ESP game

mechanics. The task for the *peek* is to guess the correct word, which is known to the *boom*, who is also given an image on which the object described by that word is. The *peek* does not see the image, but during game, *boom* may reveal him small circular areas of the image (as seen on screenshot in the Fig. 3.3) to give the *peek* hints on what word to guess. The less circles they players use to correctly guess the word, the more point they receive. Nevertheless, to be successful, the *boom* has to effectively reveal areas that contain part of the object the *peek* has to guess. According to Ahn, using the same image and tag in more games with different players and aggregating the circular areas, the obtained contours were of high precision.

Generally, we can say that the image description acquisition SAGs are capable of delivering quality descriptions and retain the quantity potential as they can be played at the same time by many players. Also the image description SAGs are in general easily transformable for video streams [17, 24]. The Ahn's ESP Game, has eventually become the best known SAG with hundreds of players every day, with claim of more than million annotated images in 3 months, which is interesting even in web scale [24], especially when the automated image categorization approaches do not work effectively.

3.2 Audio Track Semantics Acquisition Games

Another task, where semantics acquisition games are utilized, is metadata acquisition for audio resources. Similarly to graphics, sounds and music are resources represented on a sub-symbolic level which is hard to be automatically interpreted

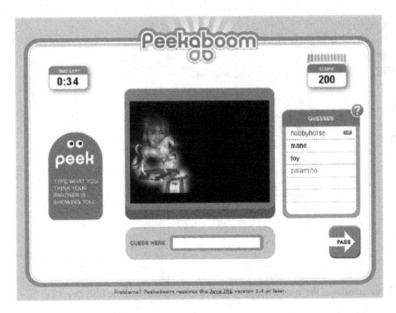

Fig. 3.3 Screenshot of the *Peekaboom* game, with purpose of identification of precise area that object occupy in the image

to symbols (e.g. a mood information about a stream of individual notes). Therefore, besides other crowdsourcing approaches, SAGs come to solve this task.

Some SAGs focus on sounds in general, other focus exclusively on music tracks, as these represent an important resource segment in information retrieval. As we mentioned in previous chapter, the spectrum of possible metadata types is wide, so SAGs for describing music can also be differentiated according to this.

A first example of a music metadata acquisition game is the *TagATune*, created by Law et al. [11]. In this game, two players hear a music track. The track may be the same for both players, or they hear two different tracks. Their task is to describe the track they hear and then decide, whether they are hearing to the same sample or not. After the game, the descriptions are collected and processed for tags (or other metadata).

An approach similar to the ESP game, but for music metadata, was created by Mandel and Ellis [12]. These authors focused exclusively on musical resources, presented to the players in 10 s slices. Their aim was to use different slices of the same song to assess changes in the music of the same track. They also devised a special scoring approach which encouraged players to enter specific tags about the song they hear: the player scores only when he enters a tag which was entered by another player *exactly* once (the game is single player). This forces the players not to enter "the obvious" tags, but rather think about more specific and rare ones (but of course, still relevant to the track). The ESP-like games on the other hand, use a word banning mechanism, which a priori declares which tags are forbidden to use for a particular image.

Different to the previous two games is the *Listen Game* designed by Turnbull et al. [20]. The difference lies in the type of the primary action that player does in the game. Instead of writing his own tags, he has to pick one which best matches the track from the list (in fact, he also has to pick a tag he considers worst). This has two effects. First, the gameplay mechanics is simpler, because the player does not have to type the words anymore, he just selects them (which is easier). Second, this effectively changes the resource description acquisition from tagging to (multiclass) categorization (with all its positive and negative effects).

A more social approach in music metadata acquisition game was applied by Barrington et al. [1] (members of the Turnbull's group). They too devised a categorization game similar to Listen Game—the players received points when they agreed on a certain answers possible to a questions they were given about the music (e.g. what is the sub-genre of the music, what is the prominent instrument playing). Moreover, the game was heavily relying on the social aspects of its players. To attract the players, the game was propagated via social networks. In addition, it kept a track about players' desires and areas of interests in the music field and matched similar players together, implying that players liking similar or the same music would also think similar about it. The authors also used these "player models" for personalized recommendation of music outside the game.

Morton et al. designed an unique SAG called *Moodswings* [14]. As its name suggest, the game focuses exclusively on the acquisition of information about the mood of played tracks (resp. the mood it evokes upon listening). In particular, the game collects the *changes* of the mood—with per-second accuracy. The players play the game in pairs and they must agree (in regular intervals) on the mood characterizing the played track (just as in ESP). An interesting feature is that players do not interact with nominal metadata values (e.g. characteristic words they would type-it or select from a list). Instead, they set the mood they perceive using a two-dimensional continuous scale on which two axes (horizontal and vertical) represent two mood dimensions: positiveness/negativeness and emotional intensity (see example in the Fig. 3.4).

Overall, the employment of SAGs in audio resource annotation and description seems to be a working idea. The approaches we reviewed deliver valid metadata of many desired types. Many reports on the existing "music SAGs" also reported that the players much liked the interaction with the music samples and the interaction with abstract symbols (tags, categories) describing them. Hearing and playing with music is a relaxing experience for them. Therefore, any music-based SAGs have an implicit advantage in this from the start.

3.3 Text Annotation Games

Description of textual documents as single entities, in comparison to multimedia description, is not so dependent on human mind labor and we are not aware of any SAGs in this field. After all, the metadata about textual documents (such as characteristic terms) are being sufficiently extracted by automated approaches.

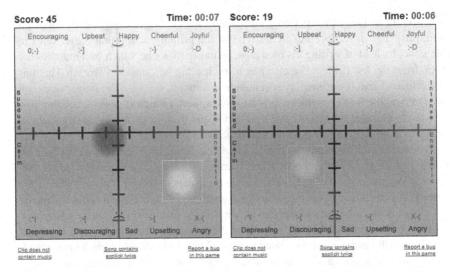

Fig. 3.4 Example of the Moodswings interface. The players are moving the cursor over the two dimensions to describe the actual mood of the music track they are listening to [14]

However, if we leave the summary characteristics of texts, there is a sentence-level text processing task, where SAGs can be and are successfully exploited: the entity co-reference identification [2, 7].

The co-reference identification has an objective to detect sets of words in the text referring to a same concept or instance. For example, in text "John was the guilty one, he threw the stone" the words "John" and "he" refer to the same subject (they are in co-reference). Such co-references are usually caused by the usage of pronouns and synonyms (mainly due to the aesthetics of the text). This however, creates an obstacle for automated text processing approaches, for example those mining the ontological facts. The co-references may span across larger portions of texts and multiple of them may overlap. All this makes co-reference identification an extremely difficult task to be solved by automated methods.

To do the job by human labor, two SAGs were devised: *PlayCoref* (by Hladka et al.) [7] and *PhraseDetectives* (by Chamberlain et al.) [2]. In PlayCoref, two players are racing in marking the co-references by matching nouns with pronouns. The player score is afterward computed by validating his guesses against the opponent and also by comparison to results of an automated co-reference detection approach [7]. PhraseDetectives is slightly different, there, the game is done in two rounds: annotation and validation (in which the opponents validates guesses of the each other) [2].

These games shows that it is not a completely bad idea to think about games for playing with text. They support the argument against the premise that there are more attractive games with rich graphical interfaces and that those games will prevail. However, the textual games may have a "rule comprehension barrier" (as stressed by Hladka et al.) because textual games such as PlayCoref or PhraseDetectives are not conventional and thus not understood intuitively.

3.4 Domain Modeling Games

Apart from resource description, several semantics acquisition games have been devised for building domain models: ontologies or other more lightweight semantic structures like taxonomies or folksonomies. These SAGs—usually word games—collect commonsense facts and transform them to ontology triplets. Some games are focused rather on validating existing facts, others solve the important task of connecting ontologies (ontology linking and ontology alignment), which is given much attention in today's research [5, 25].

3.4.1 Verbosity

For building a base of commonsense facts (e.g., "a cow is a mammal"), Luis von Ahn devised the *Verbosity* game [24]. In this game, two random partners collaborate to win, similarly to the ESP Game or Peekaboom. Also similarly to Peekaboom, the players have different but complementing roles in the game: player A is given a task term and player B has to correctly guess it.

Player A gives clues to player B. According to these clues the B has to guess the task term given to A by the game. A clue is a sentence composed by player A using one of the predefined "sentence stubs" and a word that player A may freely choose. For example, if the player A is given a task word "milk", he can construct a clue as "It is usually located in the *fridge*", "It is a *beverage*" or "It has color *white*". Such sentences effectively tell some facts about the given term, but from the game purpose point of view, they can be easily decoupled to the ontological *predicates* (equivalent to sentence stubs, e.g., "located near", "is a", "has color") and *objects* ("fridge", "beverage", "white"). If the player B guesses the given word (which serves as the *subject* of the triplet), it is highly probable that the clues (facts) provided by player A are based on widely accepted truth.

Verbosity collects such assumptions and additionally validates them by "cross-game" agreement (passing through only assumptions suggested independently by multiple players). The validated triplets are afterward added to the ConceptNet[2] ontology and available for use. The Verbosity game produces accurate facts, but it is bound by the limited set of predefined predicates.

3.4.2 GuessWhat!?

Another SAG addressing the issue of ontological relationship acquisition is the *GuessWhat!?* game [13]. The player's task is to correctly guess the concept, for which the game provides textual clues. The game is played simultaneously by two

---

[2] http://csc.media.mit.edu/conceptnet

opponents, who firstly guess the concepts and afterward evaluate the guesses of each other. The guessing is done in several rounds, in which the number and specificity of hints is increasing, so at the start, the players enter more possible concepts. The game, in fact, ends, when the number of clues is so high (they can be even contradictory) that players can no longer guess a word which suites all of them.

The interesting aspect of GuessWhat!? is that the hints are generated according to existing ontology, i.e. on the facts that are already existing and hypothetically do not need to be re-explored again. If for example, the clues (based on ontology) on the word "cat" are given (e.g.,"furry", "household" and "mammal") and the player guesses the word "cat", we have not gained any new information. However, even that is useful, because it *validates* the existing relationship. But during the gameplay, players may enter also other concepts that matches the given criteria (e.g., "dog" or "hamster") that explore new relationships. Additionally, when the game turns into evaluation phase, and players evaluate the opponent's guesses, the bad guesses that might be identified (e.g., a player writes the concept "snake" to the hint "mammal") are also recorded as invalid (the fact that snake is not a mammal may also be valuable). The authors claim the game provides valid expansion of the ontology, unfortunately, the game was not evaluated in larger scale (the authors claim only 20 players with several games played).

3.4.3 OnToGalaxy

Krause et al. created another game for populating ontology, called *OnToGalaxy* [9]. From the "purpose" point of view, the player's task is to identify *objects* matching the given *subject* and *predicate* or having a certain *property*—he does so by selecting the words matching the given conditions.

The game is interesting from the player's point of view because it encapsulates the game purpose into conventional storyline in order to make the game more attractive: it is a space-shooter game. The player is a commander of the spaceship and his task, instead of, for example: "identify all touchable objects" is more like to be "shoot down all freighters with call sign of touchable object". The player afterward selects spaceships to shoot on the screen effectively selecting objects with a "touchable" property.

3.4.4 Connecting the Ontologies: SpotTheLink

Many ontologies already exist and research issues are oriented toward finding a way of connecting them together (an issue relevant, for example, in Linked Data cloud). As we have mentioned earlier, this can be done by matching the corresponding entities in both ontologies (ontology alignment) or by identifying relationships between entities of both ontologies (ontology linking). Siorpaes and Hepp addressed this issue with the

SpotTheLink game, which is the last game in their chain of SAGs oriented on building of a commercially usable ontology [18]. Their SAGs "ontologize" Wikipedia through game *OntoPronto* and annotate Youtube videos (annotation game *OntoTube*) and Ebay offers (annotation game *OntoBay*). The SpotTheLink game is used to connect these acquired metadata to other existing ontologies.

The game principle of the SpotTheLink is as follows: The player is presented with a concept (class) of one ontology, and a hierarchical structure of another ontology where he has to identify the most suitable concept (class) and link it to the given concept with one of the predefined predicates. The more specific the predicate is, the more points he receives. The game is played by two players simultaneously, so their actions can be immediately evaluated (they have to agree). The challenging element for the players is to find a proper path in the ontology tree: they cannot see the whole tree at once, as it is too large, so they have to navigate according to descriptions of general classes (close to the root) in order to reach the more specific ones. As a by product, the quality of such class descriptions could be evaluated by analysis of the "click streams" through the tree (e.g., if the player seems to be lost in the structure, the descriptions are probably not accurate).

3.4.5 Categorilla, Categodzilla and Free Association

Next SAGs for ontology building we analyze, are the games *Categorilla*, *Categodzilla* and *Free association*, created by Vickrey et al. [21]. They do not work with heavyweight ontologies, but collect only couples of terms related hierarchically (Categorilla) or being in free, unnamed relationships (Categodzilla). Authors created these games with reference to two existing, real-life games—Scattegories™and Taboo™, assuming it will gain them some popularity (which is a interesting notion for design of the SAGs in general).

The game dynamics of the Categorilla and Categodzilla work as follows: two players collaborate and have to agree on the same output (similarly to the ESP Game [24]). Both players are given a category (concept) to which they have to match-on some subclass starting with a particular letter (e.g. for the category "bird" starting with the letter "k" the players may agree on "kookaburra"). They may enter as many words as they want, and they do not see the other player's guesses. In case of Categodzilla players type words in three separate columns (for which they are differently scored too), the first one is free word (starting with any letter), the second contains words starting with a particular "easy" letter (i.e. one that is more frequent starting letter in the language, like "c") and the third words starting with some "harder" letter (e.g., "k").

The Free Association game works similarly than games above, but with a difference: the players can type words that are in *any* relationship with the given word. They are only constrained with a set of banned words which exists to each "task" word, produced from the previous guesses. This forces players to type in words that are not so obviously related to the given word. Authors claim relatively large number of explored relationships (800 thousand raw data instances).

Vickrey et al. also made an interesting analysis of the types of the word-to-word relationships they retrieved from the Free Association (which, as we will see, is a very similar issue to one we solved in our own SAG research). Using a predefined set of possible relationships (e.g., "has", "made of" or "opposite of"), they manually typed 500 of their relationships. The most numerous were miscellaneous relationships (20 %), but synonyms and hypernyms ranked high too. An interesting option was the possible linkage of the two words with two simple relationships, through some third word (3 %). Unfortunately, authors have not analyzed the possibilities of automated relationship type mining.

3.4.6 Akinator

The *Akinator*[3] is a unique SAG for populating the knowledge base in the domain of popular or otherwise widely known persons. It is a single player game in which the artificial social agent, the *Akinator*, asks the player to secretly think of some relatively famous personage. Then, he asks the player a series of yes-or-no questions (with possible answer of *unsure-yes*, *unsure-no* and *unsure*, see Fig. 3.5).

Based on player's answers, the game filters it's existing database of persons and tries to select one that best fits the criteria given by player. Then, the game offers the player its guess (which is in many cases a correct answer—a feature that greatly attracts the players). If the player confirms the correct answer, the agent wins, otherwise, the game continues. After three wrong guesses of the social agent, the player wins. In that case, the Akinator asks the player to type in name of the person he has in mind (see Fig. 3.6). The player may also suggest a new question the Akinator should ask the players. It is also apparent that game's knowledge base and reasoning work on the probabilistic principle and is tolerant to player errors (wrong answers). If, for example, the player is having a American president in mind and answers the question "Did your character came from America" with "no", the game is able to overcome it after asking several other questions, effectively invalidating the wrong answer. From the semantics creation and the SAG design point of view, the Akinator represents a successful case of social agent backed with an existing knowledge base.

3.5 Discussion

In the last decade, we have observed proliferation of semantics acquisition games. SAGs represent a dynamic field, which firmly established itself within the crowd-sourcing research domain and the problem research domains with which the SAGs

---

[3] http://en.akinator.com/

Fig. 3.5 In Akinator, the agent asks the player yes/no/maybe questions on person characteristics

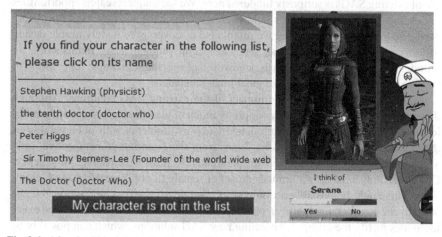

Fig. 3.6 After the Akinator agent asks a specific number of yes/no/maybe questions, he attempts to guess the person the player is thinking of (*right*). If the guess is incorrect, the agent asks the player to provide the correct answer (person), either by selecting from a potential candidates or typing in a new person

are dealing with. Mostly, these involve semantics acquisition: mainly multimedia description and domain modeling. Most of the existing approaches deliver, with high probability, the semantics with acceptable quality.

We immersed into the existing SAGs solutions from their purpose perspective (what semantics they acquire and how). For now, we left aside the design aspects of these games (although the reader might already noticed certain recurring patterns and features of the SAGs)—we cover them in the second part of this book. From the purpose point of view, the existing SAGs involve mainly creation of lightweight semantics: either description of resources with simple tags or assessing triplets under simple schemes. Only few SAGs participate in the "heavy" semantics acquisition. Still, the lightweight SAG products are useful in today's Web (which welcomes any semantics available), and so, the SAGs themselves have their place.

The existing SAG-based approaches have a certain limitation: they operate in general domain (of images, music, texts, models). It is somewhat natural: the general domain knowledge is known to many people. They can solve tasks related to it (e.g. annotate a general image, with general metadata). This makes the potential pool of players large, which means the games have larger quantitative potential and can freely use the redundant player work. On the other hand, the general domain represents only a fraction of areas where semantics are needed. These are the *specific domains* which can comprise any problem areas which somehow need to be modeled: from personal images, through very specific music genres to medical knowledge. This space is heterogeneous, but for each field, the following is valid: much less people understand it and is able to perform tasks of creating semantics for it. Therefore, the use of existing SAGs is seriously hindered here. We see major research opportunities to develop SAG solutions that would overcome this barrier. They would probably need a very specific designs, but we might also discover more widely usable design patterns which can be used to push SAGs to specific problem areas. In this work, we introduce two SAGs aimed towards acquisition of specific semantics: for creation of specific domain model and for personal image metadata.

Another question is about the impact of the existing SAG solutions. Although the existing solutions appear to cover pretty much of the semantics acquisition problems, some areas are still left untouched (such as problems with poor validity of the existing metadata on the Web). Also, from the *quantitative* perspective, only a few solutions [3, 24] managed to quantitatively justify themselves in practice. Other solutions have only a limited impact or remain in purely experimental conditions. This could be possibly accounted to many reasons (e.g. cold start problems, attractiveness, understandability), but these we analyze later. Nevertheless, the existing issues justify the efforts for creating new SAG solutions, which can possibly be more effective.

References

1. Barrington, L., O'Malley, D., Turnbull, D., Lanckriet, G.: User-centered design of a social game to tag music. In: Proceedings of the ACM SIGKDD Workshop on Human Computation, HCOMP '09, pp. 7–10. ACM, New York (2009)
2. Chamberlain, J., Poesio, M., Kruschwitz, U.: A demonstration of human computation using the phrase detectives annotation game. In: Proceedings of the ACM SIGKDD Workshop on Human Computation, HCOMP '09, pp. 23–24. ACM, New York (2009)
3. Cooper, S., Treuille, A., Barbero, J., Leaver-Fay, A., Tuite, K., Khatib, F., Snyder, A.C., Beenen, M., Salesin, D., Baker, D., Popović, Z.: The challenge of designing scientific discovery games. In: Proceedings of the Fifth International Conference on the Foundations of Digital Games, FDG '10, pp. 40–47. ACM, New York (2010)
4. Davidson, D., Davidson, D., Davidson, D. (eds.): Beyond Fun: Serious Games and Media. ETC Press, Pittsburgh (2008)
5. de Araujo, F., Lopes, F., Loscio, B.: MeMO: A clustering-based approach for merging multiple ontologies. In: Database and Expert Systems Applications (DEXA), 2010 Workshop, pp. 176–180. IEEE (2010)
6. Deterding, S., Dixon, D., Khaled, R., Nacke, L.: From game design elements to gamefulness: Defining "gamification". In: Proceedings of the 15th International Academic MindTrek Conference: Envisioning Future Media Environments. MindTrek '11, pp. 9–15. ACM, New York (2011)
7. Hladka, B., Mirovsky, J., Schlesinger, P.: Designing a language game for collecting coreference annotation. In: Proceedings of the Third Linguistic Annotation Workshop, pp. 52–55. Association for Computational Linguistics (2009)
8. Ho, C.J., Chang, T.H., Lee, J.C., Hsu, J.Y.J., Chen, K.T.: Kisskissban: A competitive human computation game for image annotation. In: Proceedings of the ACM SIGKDD Workshop on Human Computation, HCOMP '09, pp. 11–14. ACM, New York (2009)
9. Krause, M., Takhtamysheva, A., Wittstock, M., Malaka, R.: Frontiers of a paradigm: Exploring human computation with digital games. In: Proceedings of the ACM SIGKDD Workshop on Human Computation, HCOMP '10, pp. 22–25. ACM, New York (2010)
10. Larson, R.R.: Information Retrieval: Searching in the 21st Century. Wiley, New York (2009)
11. Law, E.L.M., Von Ahn, L., Dannenberg, R.B., Crawford, M.: Tagatune: A Game for Music and Sound Annotation. In: International Conference on Music, Information Retrieval (ISMIR'07), pp. 361–364 (2007)
12. Mandel, M.I., Ellis, D.P.W.: A web-based game for collecting music metadata. In: In 8th International Conference on Music Information Retrieval ISMIR (2007)
13. Markotschi, T., Völker, J.: GuessWhat?! Human intelligence for mining linked data. In: Proceedings of the Workshop on Knowledge Injection into and Extraction from Linked Data (KIELD) at the International Conference on Knowledge Engineering and Knowledge Management (EKAW), pp. 1–12 (2010)
14. Morton, B.G., Speck, J.A., Schmidt, E.M., Kim, Y.E.: Improving music emotion labeling using human computation. In: Proceedings of the ACM SIGKDD Workshop on Human Computation, HCOMP '10, pp. 45–48. ACM, New York (2010)
15. Pe-Than, E.P.P., Goh, D.H.L., Lee, C.S.: A typology of human computation games: an analysis and a review of current games. Behav. Inf. Technol. 33, 1–16 (2014)
16. Schell, J.: The art of game design a book of lenses, 1 edn. CRC Press, Boca Raton, Florida (2008)
17. Šimko, J., Tvarožek, M., Bieliková, M.: Human computation: image metadata acquisition based on a single-player annotation game. Int. J. Hum. Comput. Stud. 71(10), 933–945 (2013)
18. Siorpaes, K., Hepp, M.: Games with a purpose for the semantic web. IEEE Intell. Syst. 23, 50–60 (2008)
19. Terry, L., Roitch, V., Tufail, S., Singh, K., Taraq, O., Luk, W., Jamieson, P.: Harnessing human computation cycles for the fpga placement problem. In: Plaks T.P. (ed.) ERSA, pp. 188–194. CSREA Press, Athens, Georgia, United States (2009)

20. Turnbull, D., Liu, R., Barrington, L., Lanckriet, G.: A game-based approach for collecting semantic annotations of music. In: In 8th International Conference on Music Information Retrieval ISMIR (2007)
21. Vickrey, D., Bronzan, A., Choi, W., Kumar, A., Turner-Maier, J., Wang, A., Koller, D.: Online word games for semantic data collection. In: Proceedings of the Conference on Empirical Methods in Natural Language Processing, EMNLP '08, pp. 533–542. Association for Computational Linguistics, Morristown (2008)
22. von Ahn, L., Dabbish, L.: Labeling images with a computer game. In: Proceedings of the SIGCHI Conference on Human Factors in Computing Systems. CHI '04, pp. 319–326. ACM, New York (2004)
23. von Ahn, L.: Duolingo: Learn a language for free while helping to translate the web. In: Proceedings of the 2013 International Conference on Intelligent User Interfaces, IUI '13, pp. 1–2. ACM, New York (2013). doi:10.1145/2449396.2449398
24. von Ahn, L., Dabbish, L.: Designing games with a purpose. Commun. ACM **51**(8), 58–67 (2008)
25. Weichselbraun, A., Wohlgenannt, G., Scharl, A.: Augmenting lightweight domain ontologies with social evidence sources. In: 2010 Workshop on Database and Expert Systems Applications, pp. 193–197. IEEE (2010)

Chapter 4
Little Search Game: Lightweight Domain Modeling

Abstract In this chapter, we review our game-based approach for term relationship acquisition, called the Little Search Game. The game is in particular, focused on discovery of term relationships that are hard to be acquired by automated means. The principal game mechanics is the formulation of search queries by the player. The goal of the player is, by utilizing negative search principle (negative search terms), to reduce the result count for a given query as much ass possible. The term relationships are afterward inferred from the game logs (queries). Experiments demonstrating the relationship correctness and value, as well as their type analysis are presented. The chapter is concluded by a description of domain specific version of the game and results of its deployment.

We have devised a semantics acquisition game called the *Little Search Game* (LSG) [4]. Its aim is to contribute to the semantics acquisition field by acquiring a lightweight term relationship network (similar to folksonomy). The game was originally designed for general domain terms. Later on, we devised a modified version, called TermBlaster which aims for specific domain terms (namely for the field of software engineering education).

LSG is a single-player, competitive game of search query formulation. The task for the player is to complement the initially-given query with negative search terms to maximize the reduction of the original result set (minimize the result count). This way, he reveals, which terms he considers related to the query term. The game utilizes a search engine to call search queries and retrieve counts of results the search engine can provide. The main differences of the TermBlaster to the Little Search Game are that the player selects negative terms from preset set and that the TermBlaster's search engine operates over a closed corpus of domain specific documents.

4.1 Little Search Game: Player Perspective

The player of the Little Search Game performs game actions through extending search queries in a specific manner—using negative search. Given an initial search term (also called *task term*) to form the query, the player is asked to add *negative*

J. Šimko and M. Bieliková, *Semantic Acquisition Games*,
DOI: 10.1007/978-3-319-06115-3_4,
© Springer International Publishing Switzerland 2014

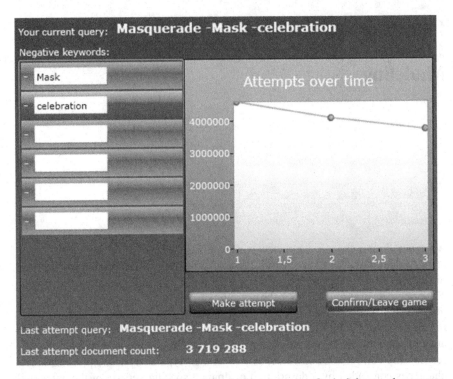

Fig. 4.1 Screenshot capturing the interface of the Little search game. On the *left* pane, player enters the negative terms. He may observe his relative progress on the chart in the *right*

search terms to it. The negative search terms (often declared in search interfaces by minus sing prefix) cause the search engine to remove all results from the query yield, that contain the particular negative search term. The player's goal, is to come up with such negative search terms (to the given task term) that will cause a *maximum possible decrease in number of results* yielded by the extended query (according to this, the player is scored). To achieve this, it is suitable for the player to use search terms *semantically related* to the query term, as these often co-occur together on the Web. The game then constructs a term relationship network by mining the game query logs.

The typical gameplay scenario of the LSG works as follows: (refer also to the game screenshot Fig. 4.1):

1. On game start-up, a task term is selected for the player, for example "star". The number of web search results is displayed for this term (it is obtained by real query). For this particular term, it is nearly 500 millions of results.
2. The player then comes up with the negative search terms, entering them into prepared text fields. For example, the player decides to use word "movie" as negative term, creating query "star—movie", because he considers these two words to be semantically related and are thus co-occurring often on the web. As a result of entering the "movie" word, the number of results drops by 100 millions

Fig. 4.2 LSG-created term network subset

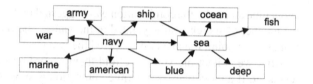

of results. The player may also observe this on the chart, showing history of the attempts.

3. The player may add more negative search terms. He may also start to change the search terms for other, to refine the query and better his results. The player may do as many attempts as he wants (until he is satisfied with his score gain, which he may review in the ladder on the right). There is, however, a limit of N negative terms (in the deployed game version, we used 6), which can be used at the same time. The number must naturally be limited, because with infinite number of terms, the game would be trivial. On the other hand, we wanted to provide some "maneuvering" space for the player, so he also could experiment with particular term combinations.

4. The game ends, when player submits the current score. He may then review overall ladder (combining results from all games played) or play another game round (with different or same term).

The winning condition—the lowest possible result count yielded—forces players to enter negative terms that have high co-occurrence with the task term on the Web, which is, due to the tendency of humans to think about the concepts, interpreted as *relatedness* of those terms. After several games were played on the same task, the agreement principle to validate answers can be applied.

4.2 Term Relationship Inference

The game rules (sourcing from the principles of negative search) force players to disclose their opinions on the relatedness of terms. When some term–term combinations are suggested by multiple players, they may become a part of term relationship network such as one depicted in the Fig. 4.2. In this section we describe the network construction, out of the raw logs of the game.

The subgroup of game logs relevant for network construction can be represented as "triplets" (p_i, t_j, N_{ij}) where

- p_i; $p_i \in P$ denotes player identifier from the set of all players P.
- t_j; $t_j \in T$ denotes task term from the set of all task terms T.
- $N_{ij} = \{n_{ij1}, ..., n_{ijn}\}$ denotes a set of negative terms used at least once by player p_i for task t_j. Also let $\forall n$; $n \in N$ where N is the set of all negative words.

These "triplets" constitute a basis for term network filtering. From them, we construct the set of term combination suggestions of a certain player, called *votes* (each vote is denoted as $l = (p_i, t_j, n_k)$ of vote set $L : P \times T \times N$). We do not consider information about time and order the combination was suggested in the game, neither we consider the number of search results yielded in the game. The only relevant information is that at some point, the player considered the two terms related.

After we collect the votes, we fold them according to term combinations they represent. If a particular term–term combination is supported by more players than specified by a threshold (a process parameter, set to 5 in our experiments), an oriented relationship is created, with task term as a source term and negative search term as target term. Moreover, each such term relationship is decorated by a ratio of two numbers, which together constitute a relative "strength" or "weight" of the relationship: the number of votes that relationship has received (ω_p) and the total number of votes that share the same source term as this relationship (ω_t).

The term network of the *Little Search Game* is then a graph G having the set of nodes V (representing terms) and set of edges E:

$$G(V, E)$$

$$V : T \cup N$$

$$E : V \times V \times \mathbb{N} \times \mathbb{N}$$

The edge represents a term relationship e; $e \in E$. e is a quartet $e = (t, n, \omega_t, \omega_p)$ where $t \in T$ and $n \in N$. The ratio $\omega_t : \omega_p$ represents the relative weight w of the edge to other edges outgoing from the same node:

$$w = \frac{\omega_p}{\omega_t}$$

4.3 Little Search Game Evaluation

4.3.1 Game Deployment

The game was deployed as a browser implementation, called Little Google Game, as it used the Google search engine to commence the game queries (yet any web search engine is applicable). The Google was our first choice (for it had broadest web space covered), but later we switched to we switched the search engine to Bing service (offered by Microsoft). We did this, paradoxically, due to the increased sophistication of the Google search, which no longer followed the Boolean logic of negative search clauses. The Bing service, on the other hand offered better results.

We deployed the game for several times. First, the game was played with an initial set of 20 arbitrary chosen task words (nouns of the common knowledge domain, e.g. "water", "castle", "brain"). Up to 300 games with 2,000 submitted queries were played by 30 players. The number of recorded logs was therefore relatively small, yet a small term network was possible to construct. It contained more than 100 terms. The players were recruited through social network.

For the sake of experimentation, to raise the number of players (and thus games played and logs collected) we opted for implementing a tournament mode of the game. Its main purpose was to bring in more incentives for potential players. In it, players compete directly over the set of same task terms. The tournament mode was put into practice at a student conference at our university, where we also awarded material prizes for the winners. Another occasion, when the game was played was during a showcase.

In total, we have recorded about 3,800 games together by 300 players, who submitted 27,200 queries. In total, 3,200 term connections were suggested (with 40 task terms featured).

The filtering procedure resulted in term network containing 400 nodes and 560 edges, yet we have to admit, that the distribution of relationship to task terms was not regular due to fact that the tournament task terms were bit "overused" by players. When we applied an additional limitation, that all, apart the 10 strongest (according to weight w) relationships per task were pruned, the resulting graph contained only 183 nodes and 220 edges.

4.3.2 Term Network Soundness

To validate the soundness of relationships in the network, we conducted an experiment with a group of judges evaluating a sample set of created relationships.

Hypothesis. Every (oriented) edge in the term network created by Little Search Game reflects a real semantic relationship of the source term with the target term. To do so, we conducted a survey evaluating the soundness of a subset of the created term network.

Participants. The survey was conducted with 18 participants of both genders aged between 18 and 30. The participants were of various professions. We considered no further knowledge about them.

Data. We randomly chose 12 relationships from the Little Search Game term network for evaluation. To create some "noise", so that participants would not realize they were expected to mark each relationship with a positive vote, we created 8 more random term pairs and shuffled them into the original 12 to create a list of 20 ordered term pairs.

Task. Participants were presented with a list of ordered term pairs, with the task: *"Do you consider the term B as being related to the term A (in other words: would you include the term B in the top 10 most related terms for term A)? (1—Definitely irrelevant, 2—More likely irrelevant, 3—More likely relevant, 4—Definitely relevant, 5—Unsure)."* We indirectly stressed the importance of evaluating a one-way relationship from A to B, since our term network is an oriented graph.

Process. All participants answered all questions. We computed whether the participants as a group rejected or admitted the relevance of term pairs based on vote counts. *Mass opinion on relevance* was set to *yes* or *no* if one of the respective weighted vote counts was at least twice that strong than the other one. The rest of the pairs was set as *controversial* and the pair was removed from further evaluation.

Results. The results have shown that nearly 91 % of the relationships in the term network were correct, which encouraged us to further research properties of the Little Search Game and the created network as well.

4.3.3 Ability to Retrieve "Hidden" Relationships

When considering the purpose of the *Little Search Game*, one may question a necessity to have a human-computation approach to acquire term relationships, when we can simply infer the relatedness from term co-occurrence (let us define the co-occurrence of term A to B as ratio of all documents containing term A and B to documents containing term A). Unfortunately, statistical co-occurrence of terms does not necessarily reflect the true semantic relatedness of terms. For example, the terms "brain" and "tumor", which are arguably relevant to each other have ten times lower co-occurrence as nonsense pair "substance—argument" (in the same corpus, the Web). Many automated approaches to semantics acquisition are threatened by some level of noise, which need to be corrected manually. In case of co-occurrence, it renders a subset of valid (semantically sound) term relationships "hidden", or indistinguishable from non-valid ones.

Fortunately, the mechanics of the *Little Search Game* allow to explore even these "hidden" term relationships (despite the scoring of the game itself is dependent on the "imprecise" co-occurrence measurement). The key force which achieves this, is the way how a regular game player thinks: although the he aims to come up with negative search terms that have high co-occurrence with the task term, he makes his guesses through the prism of true semantic relatedness. Therefore, he sometimes enters terms he consider related to task, but later he realizes, they had no effect on the result count and in next attempts, he uses them no more. However, once he used them, they remain in the game's logs, and can eventually make it through post-hoc filtering.

To confirm this hypothesis, we have conducted an experiment examining the term co-occurrence for relationships present in the LSG term network acquired earlier. Assuming the correctness of these relationships, we aimed to determine, how many of them are "hidden", i.e. are indistinguishable from nonsense relationships by their co-occurrence in a corpus (i.e. the whole Web, indexed by Bing search engine). More precisely, how many have lesser co-occurrence than "noise level" of the corpus (a co-occurrence value, which significant number of non-sense term relationships are reaching) (Fig. 4.3).

We first used the search engine to compute co-occurrence ratios for all term pairs in the LSG term network. We queried for number of results p_s containing source term (set A), then number of results p_t containing target term (set B) and then the number of results containing both terms i (intersection of A and B). Then, the co-occurrence

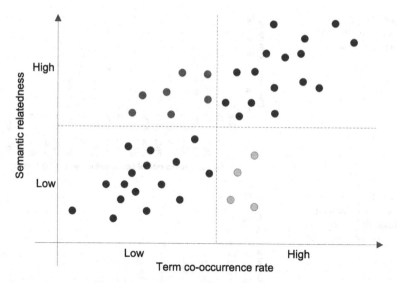

Fig. 4.3 Co-occurrence of terms not always corresponds with their semantic relatedness

ratio were defined as $r_s = i/p_s$ for source-to-target relationship (or $r_s = i/p_t$ for target-to-source). The distribution of the measured values is plotted in Fig. 4.4.

We then computed the noise level through co-occurrence of terms of nonsense pairs. We generated the nonsense pairs three times, to create three reference sets by randomly selecting them from three corpora (word sets). Each reference set contained 200 generated non-sense term pairs. The corpora contained top 800, 5,000 and 50,000 most frequently used English words (excluding stopwords). For each reference set, the co-occurrences were computed separately. Instead of one draw, we used three, because we expected, that term co-occurrence may simply depend also on term usage frequency. The distribution of the measured values for all three sets is plotted in Fig. 4.5. We can observe, how term frequency affects the distribution—while the broadest set (50,000 words), full of specific terms, scarcely crosses the 0.10 co-occurrence value, the narrowest (800) reaches even 0.5.

For final comparison with LSG network co-occurrences we used the medium sized (5,000 word) set (covering all of the terms in the LSG network). The noise for this set starts to take effect from 0.35 co-occurrence. About 40 % of LSG term network relationships falls below this this threshold, rendering them "hidden" in the noise. We can therefore conclude, that the LSG is able to help discover these relationships.

4.3.4 Network Relationship Types

The Little Search Game term network consist of terms and their untyped associations. Such structure may serve as a base for upgrading to more "heavy" structures: the

Fig. 4.4 Co-occurrence distribution of the LSG network term relationships

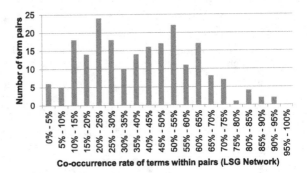

Fig. 4.5 Co-occurrence distributions of nonsense (semantically not sound) term pairs, done for three word sets

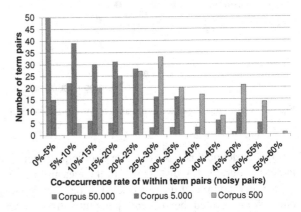

terms may be raised to concepts, the associations may be labeled with relationship types (i.e. predicates). We were interested, what types of relationships are present in term network created by LSG (e.g. are there some dominant types?). Such findings may trigger future game modifications or recommend the LSG term network as seed for other semantics acquisition approaches (out of scope of this work).

We have conducted experiments, in which we acquired types for LSG network term relationships. We did so in two ways:

1. We confronted the LSG term network with existing common knowledge base (we chose the ConceptNet ontology[1]): we took each LSG relationship's terms and queried the knowledge base, whether it contains the relationship and of what type it is. The ConceptNet defines 23 possible predicates, one of them being a general "related to" predicate. The number of predicates was suitable for our experiments, because it gave more detailed insight on the relationships, but at the same time, did not cause too much sparsity within the data.

2. Using the same set of predicates, we assigned the relationship types manually, using two judges for evaluation. As a side effect, we also re-examined the term network validity (over larger dataset, than in previous experiments).

---

[1] http://csc.media.mit.edu/conceptnet

Research questions. Is there a variety in relationship types of LSG term network? What relationship types are present there? How many of the LSG relationships are not present in the existing knowledge base?

Hypothesis. The examined relationships are semantically sound.

Data. We took 400 strongest LSG network term relationships. The ConceptNet base was accessed via online REST API.

Process. The judges (individually) evaluated each of the LSG term relationships. First they evaluated semantic soundness itself (with values 2-"strong", 1-"weak" and 0-"no"), then they assigned one of the 23 relationship types. Then, the individual contributions were merged. The soundness scores were summed. All relationships with sum equal to 4 or 3 were declared as sound, with sum equal 2 as "disputable" and others were declared not sound. When judges matched on the relationship type, the type was accepted, otherwise a general "related to" type was assigned to the relationship.

Results. The repeated soundness evaluation rendered 80 % of LSG relationships as sound, 8 % as "disputable" and 12 % as not sound. This is worse result than with our initial soundness evaluation. In this experiment however, we took more relationships including "weaker ones" (according to w value provided by the game itself). When we took only first 100 relationships (instead of 400), the "sound" portion of the set returned to 93 % (with "not sound" dropping to 1 %).

The confrontation with the ConceptNet shown, that only 41 % (164) of the 400 examined LSG term relationships were present in the knowledge base (which argues, that there is still space for finding new ways how to extend such bases).

The Fig. 4.6 compares the distribution of relationship types assigned by judges (over all LSG relationships) and distribution of relationship types assigned by ConceptNet (over those LSG relationships known to it). The LSG relationships that were recognized by ConceptNet were predominantly of 6 (of the total 23) types, while other types were not used so often. The LSG term network relationships, however, appear to have much richer distribution according to manual evaluation.

4.4 The TermBlaster

We created the game TermBlaster[2] as a modification of the original Little Search Game. By this we followed two main goals.

1. To move from domain of general semantics to a specific domain and demonstrate its semantics acquisition capabilities there. For this, we choose the domain of software engineering education.
2. Make the game more attractive to players.

---

[2] The authors wish to thank the bachelor student, Marek Kiss, for helping with implementation of the game.

Relationship Type

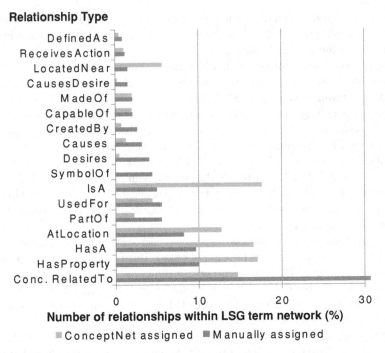

Number of relationships within LSG term network (%)

⬚ ConceptNet assigned   ■ Manually assigned

Fig. 4.6 Relative counts of the LSG relationships by their ConceptNet types and manually assigned types. Note that the scale for each of both sets is different (lesser amount of the relationships could be evaluated with the ConceptNet)

From semantics acquisition perspective, the first goal is relevant. It corresponds to one of the challenges we defined for our work: "There is still a lack of sufficient domain models, especially in specialized domains". Can a semantics acquisition game like LSG help in this? We tried it in one specific domain. A priori, we identified two prerequisites:

1. We need to switch the underlying search corpus of the game from general to specific domain documents.
2. We need to employ a group of players capable of solving the game task in the specified domain.

The first prerequisite was easily fulfilled. To switch from the general domain to software engineering education, we changed the corpus over which the game search queries are executed. Originally, it was the whole Web, now we used only documents related to the specific domain. We have obtained the documents from electronic materials of the educational system ALEF [3], available to software engineering students at our university. With document corpus changed we also needed to change the search engine. Originally, we used Google/Bing because it has whole shallow web indexed for us. Now we had to run a search engine on our own, since the materials in the corpus were not publicly available.

We were also able to fulfill the second prerequisite. Our software engineering students were at the same the target player group—they represented the "initiated" people, who have enough skill to perform well (and thus useful) in a word game in a specialized domain.

4.4.1 TermBlaster Description

We now have the underlying document corpus changed. The rest of the changes made in TermBlaster is oriented on the user interface of the game. The search queries, resp. the negative search terms are no longer entered by player as a free text, but the player picks them from a set of options. He does so by clicking on the bubbles with words, spread around two-dimensional area (as seen on the screenshot in the Fig. 4.7). We made this change to eliminate typing in the game, because it was identified by some LSG players as an interface drawback of the game, which decrease the game's dynamics.

The task for the player is formulated differently. Instead of LSG's "create a query with lowest possible result count" the TermBlaster asks the player to simply "select words that are mostly related to the given word (in the domain of software engineering)". For each word, the player receives a reward in points, proportional to the real relative co-occurrence of the given task word and selected word. This corresponds to the original LSG principle: the more are the two terms co-occurring (relatively), the more points the player receives.

Formally, let $\Omega = \{\omega_1, \omega_2, ..., \omega_n\}$ denote the domain term universum (set of terms of the domain). Then, the player solves a task defined by task term $q \in \Omega$ and a set of "option terms" $T = \{t_1, t_2, ..., t_m\} \in \Omega$. The player consecutively selects k terms from T to form $A = \{a_1, a_2, .., a_k\} \in T$. The score for each selected term a_i is computed from its relative co-occurrence with the task term. Formally, let R_t denote a result set yielded for a search query containing only term t. A partial score s_i for selecting i-th term is then defined as

$$s_i = \frac{|R_{a_i} \cap R_q|}{|R_q|}$$

where R_{a_i} denotes the result set for selected term and R_q the result set for task term. The total score s for all selected terms is then defined as

$$s = \sum_{i=1}^{k} p \frac{|R_{a_i} \cap R_q|}{|R_q|} + c_r$$

where p represents a denormalization constant (≈ 100) to make the point count larger and where c_r represents a smaller random number (≈ 10) for score blurring and adding some score for terms even not intersecting with the task term.

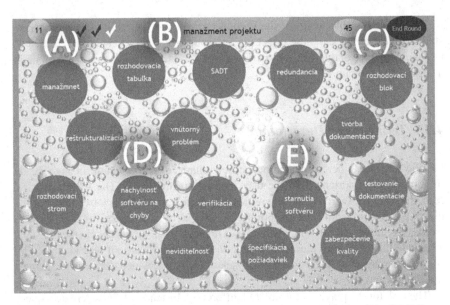

Fig. 4.7 Screenshot of the TermBlaster game interface. The player is asked to "blast" (*click*) up to three words floating in the large area (*D*) which are related most to the task term (*B*). After the player blasts a term, an information about the score for this term is displayed shortly (*E*) and score counted gets updated (*C*)

The game is played in short rounds. When the player pulls a new game, he is presented with the task term ((B), see Fig. 4.7) and up to 20 candidate negative search terms, represented as bubbles (D). The time counter starts and displays the number of seconds till the game ends (A). One game round takes 30 s during which the player has to select three of the bubbles (terms). The time stress was introduced to increase game's dynamics [1, 2]. After each selection, the player receives point count feedback (E).

After each round, the collected points are stored and used in the ladder system. The player can play as many rounds as he wants, with the same or with different task terms. However, the negative search terms are always somehow different (although they repeat after some time).

Despite the fact the interaction with the game is much more easier and the game is more dynamic (clicking instead of typing), the finite set of choices limits the player in comparison to the LSG (he might think about other terms but still can't select them). It is also apparent that the purpose of the game heavily depends on the contents of the candidate term set.

If we let the game to compose the term set randomly from the domain dictionary, we would probably end up with terms mostly not related to the task term. This way, there is a chance that the player would identify especially valuable "hidden" relationships, on the other hand, he might get frustrated from low point gains.

If we drive the selection with real co-occurrence (i.e. we offer the player terms highly co-occurring with the task term), we can mitigate the effect of frustration, because player would feel more rewarded. On the other hand if the player identifies only the high co-occurrence relationships, the game would not explore hidden relationships and would merely clear-up some noise (it can be expected that players wont pick the high co-occurrence relationships with low or no relatedness).

To find a balance between these extremes, our initial proposal was to compose the candidate term set according to real co-occurrence with three, same-sized groups:

1. High co-occurrence group. This group contains terms with co-occurrences (to the task term) above the noise level. We expected that these options would be picked the most times and would also ensure that players will not get frustrated.
2. Medium co-occurrence group. This group represents the term couples with moderate co-occurrence percentages but from the interval already spoiled by the noise. This group was the primary potential source of "hidden" relationships.
3. Low co-occurrence group, which composed from term couple with marginal co-occurrences.

The exact co-occurrence percentage thresholds between these three groups depend on the characteristics of the given problem domain. If, for instance, the domain document corpus contains many documents and relatively few terms we want to track, then the noise levels would probably be higher, than with domains with opposite parameters (especially regarding number of documents). It is therefore necessary, prior to the deployment to a specific domain, to set these thresholds carefully.

In our case (the domain of software engineering course) we have hundreds of terms we wanted to track and hundreds of documents. This resulted in the situation that most of the term couples had no co-occurrence at all and the non-zero co-occurrences were counted in units. Therefore, we decided to work with only two groups of terms, those which had and those which had not any co-occurrence with the task term.

4.4.2 TermBlaster Validation

In a preliminary experiment executed with limited number of players (38) in a period of two days, we aimed to evaluate the setup of the TermBlaster, mainly for its capability of acquiring valid term relationships. We have recorded 732 rounds played over 6 task terms (distributed equally). For each term approximately 400 terms were displayed (multiple times) as candidates and averagely 15 relationships were acquired for each (a threshold of 5 needed votes to pass was used).

The acquired term relationships were evaluated for overall soundness and whether they were of "hidden" type (i.e. they were from the "no co-occurrence" group). The soundness was firstly evaluated against existing data set—a lightweight model of the domain created for learning framework used in the software engineering course. This data set contained all terms with which the game worked (600 terms) and the relationships between them, counted 700. This however, represented only the most important relationships between the terms and not all possible, so we expected the precision to be very low. Nevertheless, we pursued the test, which rendered 21 % of relationships as correct (21 % precision with 43 % recall) and 11 % of them as "hidden".

To assess a more realistic view of the acquired relationships we also performed a posteriori evaluation, executed by three judges, which rendered 71 % of the acquired relationships as sound and 21 % of them as "hidden".

From these preliminary evaluations, we can conclude that the TermBlaster has capabilities for acquiring valid term relationships. However, in comparison to the LSG they are somewhat limited (70 % versus 91 % correctness). It also gains lesser number of "hidden" relationships than the LSG.

4.5 Discussion

With the Little Search Game, we aimed to add to the domain model acquisition with new SAG-based approach. We have deployed the game and in several experiments we validated and examined the non-labeled and non-typed term relationships it produces. We conclude them with these major findings:

- The term relationships acquired by the game were semantically sound.
- A significant portion of the acquired relationships were the valuable "hidden" relationships that are hard to be explored by automated means.
- The acquired relationships comprise non-taxonomic types (for which there is still a need in domain models), and represent an interesting corpus for further enrichment (labeling).
- With limits, the Little Search Game is able to operate over specific domain (as we demonstrated in preliminary experiments with the LSG's TermBlaster modification).

Our efforts with TermBlaster (from the semantics acquisition point of view) can be summarized as follows: The game is able to acquire valid term relationships in the specific domain of software engineering education, although with limited correctness. It also acquires some hidden relationships, despite the fact that players are no more allowed to use any terms freely, but select them from given set instead. In return for the limited correctness (which could perspectively be increased by stricter consensus measures, e.g. more votes needed for a pass) and lower "hidden" relationship gains, the game increased its dynamics and player understanding, as we assessed through informal interviews with the players.

The limited correctness of acquired term relationships in TermBlaster (relative to the LSG) could potentially be accounted to the changed interface. The combination of set of choices and time stress could force players to act more hastily. At one side, this creates a more dynamic game, on the other side, the player actions may not be so precise.

If we think more generally about the possibilities of moving a GWAP to work in specific domain, the mentioned prerequisites (to acquire specific domain semantics) appear in various flavors for all semantics acquisition games prior to their eventual use in specialized domains. For example, the ESP game for annotation of images of the architecture domain would naturally need the images from this domain only and would be need to be played only by players with some experience in architecture.

The finding of the right corpus of documents for the game (whether they are images, music tracks, texts or words) will apparently not cause much problems for the game's designer—they are almost implicitly there. The worse it is with finding of right players to do the job. For specific domain, the space is much smaller and a SAG may have much trouble attracting them and at the same time, filter out everyone else.

In case of TermBlaster, we succeeded in fulfilling the prerequisites because we knew, where to find the necessary skilled players. This is however, not possible in general. Therefore, although we succeeded in pushing an existing SAG to a specific semantics domain, we cannot claim we found an universal way to do this.

References

1. von Ahn, L., Dabbish, L.: Designing games with a purpose. Commun. ACM **51**(8), 58–67 (2008)
2. Krause, M., Takhtamysheva, A., Wittstock, M., Malaka, R.: Frontiers of a paradigm: exploring human computation with digital games. In: Proceedings of the ACM SIGKDD W. on Human Computation, HCOMP '10, pp. 22–25. ACM, New York, USA (2010)
3. Šimko, M., Barla, M., Bieliková, M.: Alef: A framework for adaptive web-based learning 2.0. In: N. Reynolds, M. Turcsányi-Szabó (eds.) Key Competencies in the Knowledge Society, IFIP Advances in Information and Communication Technology, vol. 324, pp. 367–378. Springer, Berlin Heidelberg (2010)
4. Šimko, J., Tvarožek, M., Bieliková, M.: Semantics discovery via human computation games. Int. J. Semantic Web Inf. Syst. **7**(3), 23–45 (2011)

Chapter 5
PexAce: A Method for Image Metadata Acquisition

Abstract In this chapter, we present a semantics acquisition game for image tag acquisition, called PexAce. In this game, the player's task is to (consecutively, in turns) disclose and conceal card pairs laid down on the game board, remember images on them and correctly identify identical image pairs. The game acquires the image descriptions through a game mechanics, which allows the players to make textual notes on what they see on the images. Acquired annotations are processed to tags by basic NLP and collaborative filtering. Experiments validating the game's output with a general domain image dataset are presented. Furthermore, we present a modification of the game targeted on the acquisition of specific metadata for specific images: personal photography, which is otherwise a very complicated task for either automated or crowd-based approaches.

To address the need for multimedia metadata, we devised PexAce[1]—a semantics acquisition game for image tag acquisition [2]. It is based on the popular memory game *Concentration* (or *Pexeso*), where the player's goal is to find pairs of cards (images) by continuously inverting cards on a game board. In PexAce, the players are allowed to "take notes" on the featured images to support their memory and thus provide raw-text image annotations, which, after game, are automatically processed to tags through various text processing methods. Our approach serves as a means for:

- multimedia metadata authoring via collecting and evaluating player assigned annotations into metadata,
- dynamic interactive presentation of multimedia content (typically photo albums, but it can also be extended to videos and audio),
- entertainment by engaging players by mental challenges and friendly competition.

We originally devised the approach for general domain images and metadata. As we experimented with it, we explored its potential for using it also for personal imagery, where specific metadata are needed (while there is much less approaches

---

[1] The authors wish to thank the bachelor student, Balázs Nagy, for creation of the initial concept of the game part of the method and participation on the implementation.

for their acquisition). Therefore, we devised a modification of PexAce, where players play with *their own images* and, while playing, help themselves in organizing their personal image repositories.

5.1 Description of PexAce

PexAce is a computer adaptation of the popular *Concentration* game, purpose of which is to provide annotations for arbitrary images in the form of keywords.

The original Concentration is a board card game, where two or more competing players seek for identical card pairs, contained within a pack cards consisting of several mutually different pairs. The cards are mixed and laid on the board, facing down. The players move consecutively in turns. When on turn, the player chooses and discloses (flips) two cards. If they are identical, he keeps them, otherwise he flips them back. Then the next player moves. The game ends when all cards are collected, the winner is the player with most collected pairs. Since randomly picking of the identical card pair is highly improbable (there are usually 32 pairs on the board), the only way to be successful in the game is to gradually discover and remember locations of as many cards as possible by observing unsuccessful attempts (of both player and his opponents) and then use it during one's own turns.

The PexAce is a computer adaptation of the Concentration game as well as its modification. The main shift is from multi-player to single player game with different scoring scheme. In PexAce, player gains points for every pair he discovers, but looses points for each turn he makes. He also looses (a minor number of) additional points proportional to the time spent in the game. Thus the best score is awarded to fast players playing on large board sizes (more pairs available), with economical "flip management" (good memory). The competitive aspect of the game moves from a duel to ladder ranking system, where players compete for top ranks instead of just winning a single game against an opponent.

Yet the key difference is not the single player nature of the game, but an additional feature that allow players a little "cheat" to help their memory. When particular cards are disclosed, the game allows the player to annotate the cards with textual information (see Fig. 5.1). This textual information is then available to the player for the rest of the game: the player may, at any time, hover the cursor over a disclosed card to display and read the annotation from the tooltip frame (see Fig. 5.2). This way, he may recall the position of a particular card, if the annotation he left on the card was descriptive enough.

The easier card localization motivates players to annotate images to use less number of flips and thus improve their score. It is apparent that it also lowers the original challenge of the Concentration game—the memorizing of the card positions. On the other hand, it brings a new challenge of writing effective annotations. For instance, if there are multiple similar images of beaches, a simple "beach" annotation would not properly distinguish between them, forcing players to be more specific. Only option by then is to either make extra card flips (and loose points) or use more specific annotations. Thus, especially for larger game board sizes, PexAce demands

Fig. 5.1 After flipping two different cards on the board, the player may review their larger previews and may also type their textual annotations (*center text fields*)

Fig. 5.2 When the player disclosed the first card in a turn, he may look up for the "pair" card by reviewing the annotations of concealed cards. On both screenshots, the already disclosed card pairs remain in the deck

both quality of annotations and card position memorizing since blind scanning of many image annotations still takes a lot of time (also reducing player's score).

A typical game session in PexAce is characterized by the following scenario:

1. The game is initialized with cards facing down the board, the game timer is started.
2. The player moves in turns, In each turn two cards are flipped, annotation tooltips are disabled, the timer is paused (so the player is not time-stressed during annotating), and image annotations are optionally entered for each image. Ending a turn hides the cards, resumes the timer and re-enables tooltips.
3. Prior to each card flip, players may review existing annotations by moving the mouse over hidden cards. Annotations are displayed one at a time thus the memory challenge still remains.
4. Upon finding of a pair of identical cards, it remains visible permanently, the player is awarded with points and the game passes to next turn.
5. Once all card pairs are found, the game ends. After the game, the player may review the game results: number of points, leaderboards and his rank in the ladder.

5.1.1 Image Tag Extraction

All annotations made by players are collected and stored for further image tag extraction. Because the annotations are completely free-form, the automated tag extraction process must deal with several issues. First, the annotations may contain typos or misspellings. Second, the annotations may be written in multiple languages (even for one game/player). Third, the annotation may be meaningful to the player only, e.g. due to a metaphor, not directly describing the image. Also, some words may simply be semantically wrong in describing an image (e.g. a player may misplace a jaguar for leopard).

The key overall strategy to filter out semantic noise, is to cross-validate the "tag suggestions" between players—with each annotation the player (indirectly) suggests a tag set to describe an image. But first, we must use automated means to extract these tag suggestions:

1. We use automated translation to cast all annotations to English (in our experiments, we used Google translate service).
2. We tokenize and lemmatize the annotations into tag suggestions (in our experiments, we used WordNet for lemmatization). Repeating tag occurrences are removed (only a distinct set remains).

Then, the filtering occurs: if, for an image, a tag was suggested by more than one player, this tag is assigned to the image. As the games are played, this filtering procedure is executed in regular intervals.

The cross-player filtering naturally requires that images for all games are drawn from the common image set: when a game is starting, the images used in it are drawn from much larger image pool according to some strategy. This strategy has to maximize the output of tags gained from playing (therefore, it must be greedy and prefer using same images), but at the same time, it must not "bore" the same player with same images (therefore, the same player wont find the same image in the game again, once he made an annotation to it).

The question then is, when to cease the featuring of an image in the game (when it has been "annotated enough")? For this, we used two simple rules (imposed each time after the filtering procedure has been run):

1. When number of tags acquired for an image reaches a pre-defined value (in our experiments, we used five tags), the image is no longer used in games.
2. When number of annotations made for an image reaches a pre-defined value (in our experiments, we used 15 annotations), the image is no longer used in games. This rule was introduced, because we feared that in some cases, one or few very obvious tags were used for certain images, causing the first rule to never take place.

5.2 Deployment and Tag Correctness in General Domain

We have deployed and evaluated the PexAce game with general domain images. The game was deployed as a web browser game. The acquired tags were evaluated against a gold standard as well as by a posteriori judge evaluation.

5.2.1 Game Deployment: Experimental Dataset Acquisition

For acquisition of data used in experiments, we deployed the PexAce as web browser game. As input image set, we used 5K Corel dataset, commonly used in image metadata acquisition application (the dataset comes also with a set of image tags). The game was deployed publicly, propagated through social network and word of mouth, yet predominantly, it was played by students of information technology during a tournament we organized during a conference.

The collected game logs comprised 107 players that played 814 games, in which 22,176 annotations were assigned to total 2,792 images out of 5,000 images available. The tag extraction procedures produced 5,723 tags. Out of all tagged images, 1,373 were tagged sufficiently (either received five or more tags or were annotated 15 times). For evaluation, we randomly selected a subset of 400 out of these images. The distribution of annotations was not uniform due to the greedy approach to annotation collecting.

Figure 5.3 shows how the average number of tags extracted for an image slows with constantly increasing number of annotations for that image. Because this annotation/tag number trade-off becomes inconvenient with higher numbers of annotations, a constant threshold may, in the future, be included in the strategy for deciding whether to exclude the image from the further in-game processing.

Our expectations about a lack of topic diversity in some of the images (often due to the presence of some dominant feature, e.g. an image of a horse on the meadow) were also confirmed. This can be observed in the Fig. 5.4 showing the distribution of tag count among the images annotated by same number of players.

5.2.2 Experiment: Validation of Annotation Capabilities

We have performed four experiments in which we measured the precision of the image tags acquired through PexAce. Three experiments measured precision against gold standard, fourth by a posteriori expert evaluation:

1. First, we measured precision against the original Corel 5K tags (each image has 1–4 tags per image).
2. Second, we created our own gold standard, using expert work (each image received 2–12 tags this way) and measured precision against it.

	0	1	2	3	4	5	6	7	8	9	10 Tags
1	0	0	0	0	0	0	0	0	0	0	0
2	265	143	33	9	1	0	0	0	0	0	0
3	133	113	29	12	1	0	0	0	0	0	0
4	56	62	26	6	1	2	0	0	0	0	0
5	23	33	22	5	0	7	2	0	0	0	0
6	13	23	15	13	3	11	3	0	0	0	0
7	1	17	8	3	3	24	4	0	0	0	0
8	4	9	11	7	1	30	5	1	0	0	0
9	1	10	13	15	5	34	5	1	0	0	0
10	0	16	11	12	4	35	3	3	1	0	0
11	1	8	15	5	0	37	10	5	1	0	0
12	1	5	3	5	2	39	15	0	1	0	0
13	0	3	1	2	2	47	13	3	0	0	0
14	0	0	2	2	0	45	13	5	0	0	0
15	0	26	83	155	175	75	22	10	4	1	0
16	1	8	12	32	39	24	13	7	0	0	0
17	0	4	4	14	18	7	1	4	1	0	0
18	0	0	2	5	4	3	2	1	0	2	0
19	0	1	5	2	2	2	1	3	0	0	0
20	0	1	2	6	10	3	3	0	0	0	0
21	0	0	0	7	11	2	0	1	0	0	0
22	0	0	3	3	5	2	0	1	0	0	0
23	0	0	1	3	1	1	4	3	0	0	0

Annotations

Fig. 5.3 Number of cases (*images*) where specific number of annotations (*rows*) resulted in a specific number of tags (*columns*). With the increasing number of annotations, the tradeoff for tags tends to slow. The *bottom* of the reverse "L" shaped cluster of higher values suggests, that for some images a relatively high number of annotations results only in a low number of tags (usually due to the few dominant concepts)

Fig. 5.4 There was a variety of tag counts for images that were annotated by the same number of players (in this case, 15). An effect caused by topic diversity

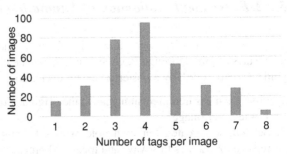

3. Third, we combined the two data sets from above (3–15 tags per image).
4. Lastly, we employed (different) experts in directly evaluating the tags produced by the game (the task for the experts was to remove wrong tags from the set).

At first, we aimed for the original Corel 5K image dataset only. It consists of 5,000 images (which we used in the game). The images are shipped with assigned tags, 65 % of images have four tags assigned. The tags are considered correct [1]. On the other hand, these metadata are very narrow—they do not even cover all major features for some of the images. Therefore, we aimed for the dataset extension by means of expert work.

Yet even the extended gold standard did not offer full coverage of topics relevant to the content of the images—many concepts have weaker links to an image content, but may still be considered relevant. The player annotators may look on the images from different perspectives, use different words even when describing the same semantics, focus on different image aspects. Therefore, we also opted for a posteriori evaluation of the created tags, which could capture the validity of all of them.

Hypotheses. The image tags acquired through PexAce are correct (they are confirmed by gold standard or experts as correct). For a posteriori evaluation, we expected a higher precision than for gold standard (experiments 1, 2 and 3) evaluation, yet for this evaluation, we expected at least 50 % precision.

Participants. The players of the game were all Slovak native speakers. They played the game mostly in Slovak language. The three experts created the gold standard, and three evaluated the game-acquired tags in a posteriori evaluation. The experts were familiar with the concept of multimedia metadata.

Data. A set of 400 images (along with their game tags) was randomly selected from images tagged within the game. Three experts working separately were asked to assign 10–15 tags for each image. When at least two of the three agreed on a same tag, the tag was added to the reference tag set of the image. The experts creating the gold standard were not aware about the tags existing in Corel dataset—these were added to reference sets afterward. In the end, each of the evaluated images had a reference set of 3–15 tags (majority of images had seven or eight tags).

Process. For experiments 1, 2 and 3, the precision was computed automatically against the reference sets. The resulting precision for each setup was computed as the average of precisions of individual images (the precision was equal to number of correct tags divided by all tags assigned to image). For experiment 4, the precision was computed in a same way—only the decision whether a tag is describing an image or not, was left to a group of judges. Each judge independently reviewed all tag assignments. When he felt a tag is incorrectly assigned, he marked it. When all judges finished working, all tags marked at least once, were considered invalid.

Results. For experiment 1 (Corel 5k dataset only), the precision was only 37.42 %, for experiments 2 (our expert gold standard) and 3 (joint gold standard), this was almost twice as much: 65 and 68 % respectively. As expected, the best results were yielded by experiment 4: 94 % precision. These results show us a high precision of the tags acquired through PexAce as image metadata.

5.3 PexAce Personal: Personal Imagery Metadata

During the deployment of the game, we observed several players during game play-ing. Besides playing (finding card pairs, annotating, running for points), they were sometimes simply watching on the images, especially those which contained some-thing unusual. They were ceasing to play for short whiles, enjoying the images. We have observed this behavior occasionally during the experiments with the Corel 5K image dataset, but more often this occurred later, when we used the game just for showcasing it at various events. Then, rather the general domain images, we used photos with which many of the players were familiar—past year photos taken on the same occasion. The game acted also as a image presentation tool. And familiar images made it more attractive.

This suggested the idea to use the game to annotate not just any images, but images familiar or personal to the player himself. Also, and more importantly: the purpose of the game would become useful for the player himself. It would help to acquire metadata useful in maintenance of personal image repositories (e.g. family photos). This is an unpopular and tedious task, which at the same time, cannot be currently done by other means than manual work of the image owner himself. The trouble here is with the highly specific metadata: names of persons, places or events connected to the images—something that neither crowd or automated method could provide.

We have examined the practices of users in dealing with personal imagery orga-nization. As a main source, we used the qualitative study of Vainio et al. [3], which analyzes the prevailing practices of multimedia resource creators and users (of mainly images), in regard to the metadata creation and upkeep. According to this study, users like to interact (create and edit) with the content (of the images), but not with its meta-data, although their recognize their importance. Even when they admit, they have trouble with organizing of their repositories, they are not willing to spent time on metadata creation. The only common practice is the high-level hierarchical organi-zation of resources into named albums. Apart from this, the retrieval process relies on chronological sorting and extensive thumbnail browsing.

For us, this represented an opportunity to bring in an alternative solution for acquiring personal imagery metadata. The idea of this game was that players would play the semantics acquisition game with their own images and keep the acquired metadata for their own sake.

One of the important notions of the Vainio's study was, that users would mostly welcome specific metadata to describe their resources: person names, places and events where pictures were taken. Therefore, for our own study, we were especially interested in the game's performance in acquiring these types of metadata.

To achieve our goal—*acquire personal imagery metadata through semantics acquisition game*—we modified the original PexAce into a game called *PexAce-Personal*. From the player's perspective, the gameplay was kept in its original form. The only change was the image dataset loaded into the game—prior to the game start, the player loads his own image set.

However, the original tag extraction procedure rely heavily on the cross-player validation. It needs a substantial number of players playing the game with the same data set. But such pool of players is not available in this case, because the specificness of the desired metadata narrows the group of people able to provide them. This is an disadvantage of any crowdsourcing process aiming for a specific information acquisition. Overcoming it may include increasing worker motivation and finding alternative ways to validate the produced information. Our solution utilizes both.

Concerning motivation to play, the PexAce-Personal comprises three motivational aspects:

1. The original game challenge (e.g. finish the game, beat the highest score). Interestingly, even when the players play with different image sets, their mutual comparison according to score is possible, because the scoring is in fact independent on the actual image content.
2. Interaction with familiar content. While playing, the players experience the pleasure of reviewing their images, especially those they have not seen for longer time.
3. The players that are aware of the game's purpose know that they are helping themselves or their relatives or friends. This strengthens their motivation for participation.

Motivated players, aware of the game's purpose would produce more accurate and specific annotations. This allows us to rely more on the sole player tag suggestions and lowers the need for cross-player tag validation. This is very convenient for the use case, because we can expect that in some cases, only one player will be available to play with one image set (although the game encourages player to "share" it among friends, to "help him by playing"). Thus, the images used in the game are personal images of the player or belong to his social circle.

The original cross-player tag validation was complemented with several less restrictive heuristics enabling the game to accept tags entered by only one player. They also optionally exploit a common album-like groupings of images in personal repositories.

The pre-processing of the annotations created in the PexAce-Personal is executed in the same manner as with the original game. The texts are tokenized and lemmatized, the stopwords are removed. The only difference is the missing automated translation to English, which we omitted in this case, since it would be too inaccurate for specific texts (often containing metaphorical references). The natural language processing procedures were therefore implemented for each language separately and the players were asked to explicitly select their game language (for the experiments described below, we used Slovak language).

As with the original approach, the output of pre-processing were tag suggestions triples—*player-image-tag*. In PexAce-Personal, we add a fourth element to the suggestion, the identifier of *album*, in which the image was present (an information often available). When the album information is not available, the validation heuristics utilizing it are not applied. The set of the tag suggestion quartets (player-image-tag-album) are subject to the following filtering heuristics:

1. When two or more players agree on the same tag over a single image, that tag is declared valid. This is the original cross-player scheme. When the pool of players is very narrow, it becomes very restrictive (although it is precise). Yet with the additional player motivation and purpose awareness, it might be considered unnecessarily strong, so we introduced several "weaker" ones.
2. When the same player repeats a certain tag for a given image (which may happen if the image is used in more than one game), it is declared valid. The repetition of terms (even by a single player) may indicate that their use was not a mistake.
3. When the same tag was used (sufficient number of times in total) by one or more players to describe various images within the same album, all of these tag assignments are declared valid (the "sufficient" value used in our experiments was four). This rule takes advantage of the possible recurrence of same concepts within a single image album, such as person names.

5.4 PexAce Personal: Evaluation

We have performed a combined quantitative–qualitative study to evaluate the PexAce-Personal. The study included the gameplay itself, so no prior game deployment was performed. We examined:

1. Validity of the image tags acquired through game.
2. To what extent are these tags "image-owner-specific".
3. The types of tags extracted as well as performance of the game over different types of images.
4. How the game performs, when players are unaware of its purpose (with respect to the possible scenario of sharing the game within one's social circle).

Research questions. We have defined following research questions, under circumstances that the game is played with low number of players with their personal images.

1. Do tags describe the images correctly (measure of correctness (precision)—a ratio of correctly assigned tags to all assigned tags)?
2. How specific (to the social group, to which the images belong) are the correctly assigned tags (specificity)? How are the tags understandable (to persons outside the social group) (understandability)? The understandability (for "outsiders") is a minor factor for us, yet it says something about the usefulness of the tags. We expected the understandability to be inversely correlating with specificity.
3. What effect does the awareness about the game's purpose have on the measured characteristics and the perception of the game by players?
4. In what quantities are the following metadata types—person names, places and events—present in the acquired tag sets?
5. For which type of images is the approach suitable. We have defined several image categories orthogonal to their topics: portraits, groups, situational (may contain persons, but the dominant feature is some situation) and no-persons images.

Participants. In this study, we used two groups of participants with each having four members. The purpose of having two groups was to observe the influence of awareness about the game's purpose (one group was told that they are creating metadata for their images, the other not). Each group comprised members of the same social group, which has several common interests as well as images. Two of the participants in each group were *players* in this study, one served as a tag evaluation *judge* and one helped in preparation of the image set prior to the playing (*preparator*).

Data. Each preparator created a set of 48 images to be used in the game. Images were drawn from a larger pool comprising three albums. The members of preparator's group were familiar with the contents of the images. The preparator drawn 12 images for each of the defined categories (portraits, groups,...).

Methodology and process. The players played the game individually, under our supervision. The playing was followed by an interview. First, the players rules and features of the game were explained to the players. Then, for one of the groups, the purpose was explained. During the gameplay, the players were allowed to comment their actions, if they considered it necessary. After the gameplay, we asked them to comment on the game in general. All answers were recorded and analyzed post hoc.

Each player played three game rounds, with different board sizes: 6×6, 8×8 and 10×10 cards. Each card pair of the 48 pairs was featured twice in the game. For the 10×10 game the remaining two pairs (48 was not enough to cover 100 card slots) were selected randomly and were not considered in the evaluation.

After the game sessions, the tag extraction was automatically run and the tags were prepared to be evaluated by judges. For this, we implemented a simple application, where images were consecutively presented with their assigned tags and judges were asked to fill in the information about them. Prior to this, the judges were introduced to the concept of multimedia metadata (need for their creation and ways of use). They were not introduced to the game itself. For each assigned tag, the judges had to answer the following:

- Is the tag describing the image correctly?
- In case of correct tag, is it specific for the group (i.e. do you think it is possible, that a person not familiar with your group would be able to provide this tag)?
- In case of correct tag, is it understandable for people outside your group?
- In case of specific tag, assign one of the following type: person, place, event or other.

Results. For both groups together, 366 tags were extracted by the filtering heuristics. From this number, only one third (122 tags) passed according to the cross-player validation rule. The rest passed by second (repeated use of a tag on an image by single player, 196 tags) and third rule (repeated use of a tag for an album). This demonstrated a substantial increase in quantity of acquired tags through less restrictive heuristics. There was also a significant difference between the quantities of tags between the participating groups: the purpose aware group provided annotations, from which 2.5 times more tags were extracted, than from the purpose unaware group logs.

The overall correctness of the acquired tags was 90 %. Here, a difference between the two groups was noted: 96 % for the purpose aware and 86 % for unaware group.

With these results, we consider the approach to be delivering valid tags in general. From the correct tags, the judges identified 38.5 % to be specific. Here, the groups also differed: the purpose aware group players provided 44 % and unaware group 33 % of specific tags. Considering this, we can conclude, that our approach is also able to acquire the valuable specific information for personal archives.

Overall, we can conclude, that the PexAce-Personal gameplay was capable to deliver valid metadata for the featured images, partially also specific for the needs of personal image repositories. The results also shown that all players were able to deliver a valuable output regardless of the awareness about the game's purpose, however, we have also observed quantitatively and qualitatively larger contribution from purpose aware players. Only in case of understandability the "unaware" group performed better (which was according to our expectations). A typical case of correct specific but "not-understandable" tag was a name of an event to which some images were related. From this, we conclude, that making the players aware about the game's purpose makes a significant positive impact on the quality and quantity of acquired tags. We attribute this to the combination of this awareness with the motivation of "working for oneself". On the other hand, the purpose aware players reported that they were also less enthusiastic about the gameplay and the focus on the providing better annotations distracted them a bit from the gameplay fun.

The follow-up analysis shown that the specific tags contained (were of type):

- 53 % person names,
- 21 % event,
- 15 % places,
- 11 % other.

The "other" typed tags mostly have humorous connotations, as reported by judges. This shown, that the players like to entertain with the annotations themselves. The humor is probably also the reason for relatively outstanding difference between tag specificity levels delivered by players of different groups for situational image category: while for the purpose unaware players, this was a perfect occasion to make jokes in the annotations, the purpose aware group was more disciplined. The groups were much more coherent (in terms of specificity) in case of portraits and group photos. The worst specificity results were achieved for images not containing persons. This suggests that in future use, the game might utilize an automated method for person presence detection in the images loaded to it, in order to increase its usefulness, in terms of tag specificity.

Lastly we have qualitatively analyzed the session records, namely the player verbal expressions about the game. As most important, two notions were recurring. As a positive outcome, the players reported, that they enjoy playing with their own images, especially longer unseen. On the other hand, players were skeptical about the repeated use of the same images in multiple games player shortly after each other. They were confused during the gameplay, unsure whether the image they have just seen, they recall from the actual or past game. They have also reported, that they tend to use exactly same annotations for them(which may cause a lack of tag diversity for certain images). Thus, for future use of the game, the image selection heuristics responsible for game round setup, would have to respect the past occurrences of images and select them again only after longer time periods.

5.5 Discussion

To address the challenge of lack of multimedia metadata (particularly for personal repositories), we devised semantics acquisition games of PexAce and PexAce-Personal. With their game log processing procedures, we presented a working approach for acquisition of descriptive image tags. After the controlled and uncontrolled deployment and experiments with the game, we can conclude:

- Our approach is capable to deliver valid metadata (tags) for general domain of images.
- When used over personal image collections, the approach retains its levels of tag correctness, even when only very low number of players is participating on gameplay over the same image collection.
- Furthermore, the game yields desired types of metadata needed for personal collections such as person names, places and events.

Although the overall precision of the method is good, there are several secondary issues, solution of which would improve the output of the game (qualitatively and quantitatively).

As one source of bias, we identified the automated translation of annotations to a single language. In particular, this was a problem for shorter annotations, where the automated translation service could not exploit the word context in case of homonyms. Moreover, in our particular experiments, where most of the annotations were done in Slovak language, more bias was introduced by the lack of proper accents in texts, which may significantly change the meaning of individual words. The solution for this may be to restrict the game language (and annotations) to English only, however, we have concerns about the possible distraction of some players. As a supporting mechanics to this, may be the auto-complete text typing functionality (e.g. as in search engines).

This would proactively suggest English words or even concepts (if the auto-complete box was backed by a domain model) and reduce the bias. A downside of such approach though, would be probable inefficiency of "general English" dictionary in "personal" version of the method (as many player-specific words would be used in the game). On the other hand, a specialized gazetteer might prove useful here (e.g. a list of player's friends, some of which could be expected in the images, could be acquired through player's social network identity).

Another feature of the method that can be improved is the player "work" allocation, i.e. what image is assigned to which game, resp. its effectiveness. In other words for a constant number of player inputs, we want to maximize the output of the game, i.e. the number of correct tags. The factor that influences this effectiveness ratio is the decision when to suspend an image from occurring in the games. In our experiments, we used a rather naive approach: an image is featured within the games until the number of its annotations reaches 15 or number of its output tags reaches five.

Although this was sufficient for executing our experiments and for proving the method concept, in practice, such approach introduces several types of events which may occur during the annotation process and which cause that human work is used inefficiently. They would mostly be caused by semantic characteristics of each individual image, namely the number and relevancy of concepts related to it.

- When an image has only few dominant concepts related to it, the players would probably use only these in their annotations. This "low tag diversity" would cause that many annotations would be unnecessary redundant (repeating the same tags) and neither output tag count or annotation count threshold would prevent "wasting" of the player "work" which could be used elsewhere.
- When the number of concept related to the image is high (with no "apparently dominant" concepts) the tag suggestions of the player crowd become more diverse. This can cause a situation, when many "good" tag suggestions remain unconfirmed by other players upon reaching the annotation count threshold.

In the future, a possible solution to this problems may lie in a more dynamic approach based on some diversity measurement metric used for making decisions about annotation suspension. Moreover, in case of "high tag diversity problem" a new game mechanics could possibly be used: assuming that players suggest many tags to an image (not yet validated by other players), the game could use these to "auto-tag" the image for the player. This way, they could validate the existing tags instead of creating new ones. The positive or negative outcome of the validation would be determined by the player behavior: either he would make mistakes using the auto-tagged image (which would indicate that the tag is wrong) or he would successfully use it to find pairs (in this case, the featured tags would probably be right).

References

1. Ke, X., Li, S., Cao, D.: A two-level model for automatic image annotation. Multimedia Tools Appl. **61**, 195–212 (2011)
2. Šimko, J., Tvarožek, M., Bieliková, M.: Human computation: image metadata acquisition based on a single-player annotation game. Int. J. Hum. Comput. Stud. **71**(10), 933–945 (2013)
3. Vainio, T., Väänänen-Vainio-Mattila, K., Kaakinen, A., Kärkkäinen, T., Lehikoinen, J.: User needs for metadata management in mobile multimedia content services. In: Proceedings of the 6th International Conference on Mobile Technology, Application & Systems, Mobility '09, pp. 51:1–51:8. ACM, New York (2009)

Chapter 6
CityLights: A Method for Music Metadata Validation

Abstract This chapter presents our semantics acquisition game called CityLights and experiments related to it. It has the purpose of validating of existing tags for musical resources in datasets where tag quality (correctness, descriptiveness) is not ensured. The game has a form of music quiz, where player first hears a music track and then he is asked to select one of the prepared tag sets, which best characterizes the music track. The tags that mostly confuse players (lead them to false answers) are declared invalid (and are removed from the dataset).

A general need for metadata exists also in the domain of music multimedia resources. Music metadata comprises a wide range of types such as author and interpret of the music, creation or recording year, genre, mood, lyrics theme, place where the music should be listened, rhythm, tonality etc. Some of these metadata are generally provided by the resource creators, other may be inferred automatically [1, 4], but as with many other multimedia, a human (crowd) labor [2] is needed to acquire all types of metadata for music tracks.

The existing approaches result into a solid quantity of metadata available for musical resources. However, the quality of these metadata is unreliable. Users introduce a lot of noise to the tags, contributing with subjective descriptions and sentiment. They may also assign wrong tags (such as genre). A simple crowdsourcing principle: a cross-user validation results in a very limited set of metadata (mostly tags). A noise is also introduced by automated metadata extraction methods. During our experiments with the LastFM corpus, we have identified that more than a half of its tags was assigned wrongly or with very weak connection to the music tracks.

In such conditions, the music metadata acquisition problem turns into the validation problem: rather than creating new metadata, we need to validate the existing sets to re-rank them and filter out those incorrectly assigned.

The music metadata validation is the task for our method and a SAG called CityLights [3]. The game works with real data corpus—the LastFM tag database.

The authors wish to thank the bachelor student, Peter Dulačka, for participation on the design, implementation and validation of the game

J. Šimko and M. Bieliková, *Semantic Acquisition Games*,
DOI: 10.1007/978-3-319-06115-3_6,
© Springer International Publishing Switzerland 2014

From the player's point of view, it is a simple question answering game: the player hears a music track and has to decide, which of the presented tag sets was originally assigned to that music. By tracking his behavior and behavior of other players at the same question, the game is able to assess the correctness of tag assignments.

6.1 CityLights: Method Overview

The CityLights is a SAG and a method for metadata validation. Though we demonstrate it for a music domain, it can be analogically used for other types of multimedia metadata validation (e.g. tags assigned to images) or for validation of multimedia relationships to other multimedia (e.g. images assigned to music). As input it takes the multimedia (music tracks) with existing metadata with uncertain quality (textual tags), and outputs the validity ratings for the provided input metadata.

The basic task that player solves in the game, has a form of a choice question: the player is presented with the multimedia sample (he hears the music) and a set of choices, one of which he is asked to pick. The choices are sets of tags. One of the choices (the "correct" choice) is composed of tags that have been assigned to the actual music track in the input corpus. Other choices consist of tags assigned to different music tracks in the corpus. The player is asked to pick the "correct" tag set (i.e. the one that originally belongs to the music track). If he succeeds, he receives points, if he picks a wrong one, he looses them (he bets score points).

By answering the music questions described above, the player gives us the information on the validity of the presented tag assignments: if he answers a question correctly, it can be assumed that some of the tags of the choice he picked somehow describe the track that he hears. If he answers incorrectly, then the descriptive value of the tags in the "correct" choice is limited. By consecutively repeating the same (or similar) question for multiple players, the personal views of the player become the crowd "wisdom", ruling out or confirming individual tags.

The game uses a simple storyline metaphor: the player travels through a city (depicted in the Fig. 6.1) and at each crossroad, he has to choose the right way. This pick is represented by the musical question. In the simple game interface, the player has a music playback controller (left), a map of the city (center) and a choice viewer (right), where he can review the choices by hovering over the alternative ways in the map. Before each choice pick, the player must bet a certain number of points in Fig. 6.2. After the correct choice, the player doubles the bet points and continues to the next crossroad (question), until he reaches the end of his way through the city.

6.1.1 A Music Question Example

Consider the following example: the player hears a well-known sample of the Beethoven's *5th symphony*. Along with it, he is presented with three choices (each composed of a random subset of tags found in the input corpus):

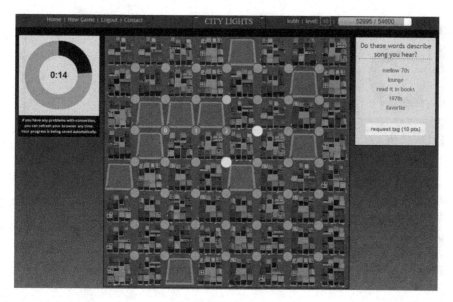

Fig. 6.1 An example of the CityLights game interface

1. (a "correct" choice composed of tags) *lovely*, *19th century* and *classic*.
2. (a choice composed of tags belonging to Beethoven's *Egmont* overture) *Beethoven*, *classic* and *dramatic*.
3. (a choice composed of tags belonging to Mozart's *Turkish march*) *march*, *funny* and *piano*.

The setup of this question is a bit tricky for the player. At first, the "correct" choice is composed of quite "unfortunate" tags. The tag *lovely* is very subjective and objectively has no distinctive power. The *19th century* tag is correct, but very general and the *classic* tag, though correct in a broader sense (classical music), is in fact wrong, because the piece belongs to the romantic period (rather than classical).

On the other hand, the second choice looks much more promising. The *Beethoven* is a strong clue, valid not only for the second choice, but also for the first. Also, the tag *dramatic* characterizes the *5th symphony* as well as *Egmont overture*. The third choice is in this case a very distinct to what the player hears, but the second choice looks most promising, so player picks it.

After the wrong choice pick, the player looses some points and can pick again. Now, he has a good chance of picking the "correct" (i.e. the first) choice. The player might be confused by the outcome of his first answer, but he knows about the nature of the game, e.g. that he is dealing with a noisy dataset. He simply follows the game task: identifying the original set. By choosing the wrong choice first, however, he indirectly indicates that the tags present in the wrong choice are comparably better describing the played track that those in the first choice. If the player, on the other hand, would pick the correct option first (perhaps in a different question), he indirectly states that out of the present choices, these tags represent the music track best.

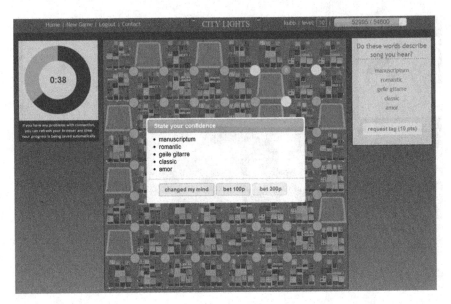

Fig. 6.2 The CityLights game interface after the player chooses one answer option. Before confirming the choice he may once again review the tags it contains, set the height of the bet or take his decision back

The "unfortunate" circumstances for the player in terms of drawn tags can occur quite often if the input metadata corpus is of bad quality. From the game perspective, it is important that the player encounters a balanced portion of "easy" or "not tricky" questions to the "unfortunate" questions such as the one with the *5th symphony*. The player must not get bored, but also not get overwhelmed.

6.1.2 Validating Individual Tags

So far, we know that each player answer represent a relative comparison of two groups of tags (in terms of their correct assignment). At the start of the crowdsourcing process, each of the tags present in the input corpus is assigned with the *support* value, which will later act as a sum of positive or negative feedback acquired via player interactions with this tag. Using the example from the previous Sect. 6.1.1, when player selects the wrong choice, each tag in the "correct" option has its *support* decreased (because they were not convincing). On the other hand, if the player selects the "correct" choice, all of its tags will have its *support* increased. We define two thresholds (positive and negative) that define at what values, the *support* marks a definitive correctness: when the *support* value of a certain tag reaches one of the pre-defined thresholds, it is declared as confirmed or rejected tag. Alternatively, the support value may also act as a property of ranking the tags assigned to a single music resource in the input dataset.

However, in order to validate the tags in the dataset, we need it for *individual* tags, not groups of tags. The individual tag validation is achieved by *variation* in the game question composition. For each question that features the same track, the subset of it's original tags is always different, causing a variation in the descriptiveness of the whole choice set and therefore, a space for really good, descriptive tags to "prove" their power.

This variation effect is best illustrated by an example: consider a music track decorated with 4 tags within the input dataset: *nice, awesome, Beethoven* and *classic*. Consider that only the *Beethoven* tag is assigned correctly, while other tags are subjective or vague. The question featuring this particular track appears 4 times in the game, each time with a different 3-member subset of the tags above:

1. Beethoven, awesome, nice
2. nice, classic, Beethoven
3. awesome, classic, Beethoven
4. awesome, nice, classic.

Suppose the tag *Beethoven* (featured in the first three occurrences of this question) has a sufficient descriptive power that it convinces players to pick the presented tag set each time as a first choice. Each time this happens, all of the tags presented in the choice will have their support increased. However, when the fourth option comes by, the player will not select it (because of the vague and non-descriptive nature of its tags) and will select another choice instead. Therefore, after all four combinations, the truly correct and descriptive tag *Beethoven* will have a higher *support* value, than the other tags.

A valid design question with this game might be: why did we chose to compose choices of multiple tags, and not single tags? The answer is a practical one: with only one tag, the game would be hardly playable for the player. A high number of wrong or noisy tags would make the guessing very hard or a not challenging random betting. If the player has more tags in each choice (in our experiments, we used 5), he encounters "good" ones more easily and has therefore more successful attempts.

6.1.3 More on the Game's Features

The basic choice question task forms the core element of the CityLights SAG. It is, however, complemented with other gameplay features that enhance the metadata validation abilities of the game and encapsulate its purpose into the storyline.

Explicit tag "rule-out"

The question answering can be considered as a form of implicit user feedback on the validity of the featured tags (the player solves different task from which the validity is inferred). However, we also offer the player to rule out the wrong tags explicitly. For a small point reward, the player has an option to mark tags that confused his decision making:

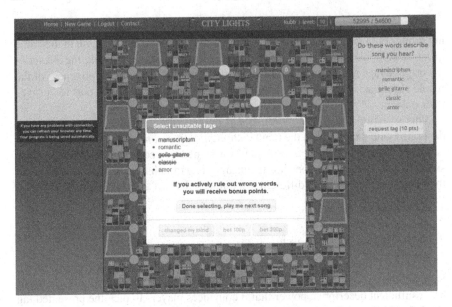

Fig. 6.3 The CityLights game interface after the correct pick. The player just explicitly ruled out two tags that he considered invalid

- After a "correct" choice pick, the player can mark a tag (or more) within the "correct" choice tag set that he considers being wrong or of no value (see Fig. 6.3). The player is rewarded by a *constant* minor point gain (regardless on the number of tags he rules-out). The constant value is to reduce the motivation to abuse this feature to gain more points. Secondly, we also motivate the player to rule-out the tags correctly: the tags he rules out will not appear in the game for the current music track anymore for that player (the player may encounter the track more times). Therefore, a correct "cleansing" of the tag sets is also in the player's interest.
- After an incorrect choice pick, the player can mark tags within the selected choice which convinced him to guess wrongly. Later, these tags may become candidates to be added to the description of the played track, even if they were not present there in the input set. (In the current implementation of the CityLights, we have not included this option—it is a subject for future work).

Tag buying

Another minor feature of the CityLights is the so called *tag buying*. In the game, players often hesitate between several choices or are unable to assign any of the choices with the currently playing music. In both cases, this means that the quality of tags in the "correct" choice might not be ideal. It is therefore convenient to measure this type of feedback. Even though the player "hesitation" could be implicitly assessed by measuring the time between the question stating and answering, we came up with a more explicit form of feedback.

For each choice, the player can uncover few more tags for a small point fee (in our experiments, where the original tag count per choice was 5, the players might uncover 3 more tags). These tags are drawn from the input corpus and may eventually help the player in solving of the question. However, by requesting for more tags, he also expresses his confusion with the current state of the question, which can be taken into consideration in the tag *support* value changes after the question was answered.

Besides it has value for the tag validation process, the *tag buying* contributes to the playability of the game as is decreases the danger that the player might get distracted after encountering several "hard" questions. With more tags, his chances to answer the question correctly increase. To further assure this effect, the last of the additional tags the player can request for a single choice is drawn from the correctly or near-correctly assigned tags belonging to the music track the choice belongs to. This way we aid the player by introducing quality tags to him.

The city metaphor and traveling through graph

A game session of the CityLights is a sequence of music questions as described above (along with the minor features of *tag buying* and *explicit tag rule-out*). This sequence however, is graphically represented by a graph—a city with a square-based grid, where crossroads represent individual questions in Fig. 6.1. As player answers the questions, he travels through the graph as a metaphor of the street-walking.

The metaphor has no particular effect on the game mechanics (except the fact that the player may encounter several "incorrect" choices, resp. crossroads multiple times), however, it helps to encapsulate the game's purpose and gives the game a little background story. This story is also emphasized by the overall visual design of the CityLights that evokes a city in the night.

6.1.4 Realization of the CityLights

The method (resp. its realization) consists of a game part and an analysis part. The *game* part is a web-based application, in which the player plays the game (with all the features described above). The product of the game part are the game logs containing all the relevant information needed for tag validation: the overall game setup, questions and choices, player guesses, tag purchases, rule-outs, etc.

The *analysis* part consumes the logs and process them to produce tag validity indications through modification and evaluation of the *support* value. Moreover, it feedbacks the game part with the information on which tags/tracks should be excluded from further playing (e.g. they have been validated), or which should be played more often (e.g. are close to be validated).

In the sections above, we have described the principles and situations of changing of the *support* value of the tags assigned to multimedia resources. In this section, we describe them once again in a more rigorous manner.

For the tag evaluation process through the *support* value, we have identified several parameters that can influence the outcome (correctness and "labor effectiveness") of our method. Somehow, we had to decide about the right values for various action weights and thresholds so the method could correctly evaluate the featured tags for a minimum number of player's actions. Therefore, we decided to firstly set them by hand, collect the dataset of the game logs, and then, using simulations, tune the parameter values for best performance. Also, as a part of our method, we created the combinations of parameters with the input values (computed from game logs). These expressions were firm, and have not undergone changes.

We have identified following parameters, input values, constants (parameters that have not been a subject of training) and variables that feature in our tag validation mechanism:

- *support*—a tag validity *support* variable itself. At the start of the process, it is set to zero.
- $\Delta support$—a change of the *support* value.
- ε_{upper}—a threshold of the *support* value, a positive number and a constant. If support reaches this value, the tag is confirmed as correct.
- ε_{lower}—a threshold of the *support* value, a negative number and a constant. If support reaches this value, the tag is rejected as incorrect.
- *nbr*—A number of choices available at the time of the player action.
- *attm*—A number of player attempts in this question, including the current action.
- *conf*—A confidence of the player. A number between 0 and 1, where 1 corresponds to the highest possible bet.
- ans_c—A weight of the support change in case of "correct" choice was picked.
- ans_w—A weight of the support change in case of incorrect choice was picked.
- tag_c—A weight of the support change in case when player selects a possibly correct tag in a wrong choice.
- tag_w—A weight of the support change in case when player rules-out a incorrect tag in the "correct" choice.
- *buy*—A weight of the support change when player buys an additional tag (the change affects the other tags present in the choice).

The latter five are the parameters to be trained. The following are the situations, where the *support* value is altered due to the player's action:

The player chooses a "correct" choice

The positive *support* change. It is influenced by player's confidence and number of other choices (the higher, the harder is the question). Also, the positive impact is exponentially decreased when the choice was selected after more attempts.

$$\Delta support = \frac{ans_c * conf * nbr}{2^{attm}}$$

The player chooses an incorrect choice

The negative *support* change. Unlike in the previous case, the impact is decreased by the number of other choices.

$$\Delta support = -\frac{ans_w * conf}{nbr}$$

The player rules-out a tag after a "correct choice".

$$\Delta support = -tag_w$$

The player marks a positive tag after an incorrect choice.

(was not included in the game release).

$$\Delta support = tag_c$$

The player buys a tag

(was not included in the game release).

$$\Delta support = -buy$$

The important question about the validation process is: when the validation of a single tag ends? Naturally, it ends after its support reaches one of the thresholds. However, this may take a long time even if the tag retrieves a lot of feedback, because the individual feedback actions might be contradictory. Ultimately, the tag might circulate in the game forever, "wasting" the power of the crowd. Therefore, we chose to put the tags out of the game after a critical number of feedback actions has affected it, reaching neither upper or lower threshold. This critical number was a constant which we handpicked as a estimated number of feedback actions needed for a very good or very bad tag multiplied by ten. Tags that have been drawn out of the process this way, were declared as "not confident" cases.

6.2 Experiments: Evaluation of the Metadata Validation Ability

To validate our approach, we have developed and deployed the CityLights as a web application and conducted an open, unsupervised experiment with real users. We then computed the correctness of the tag validation (against the expert validations in the same corpus). Then we conducted the simulations to achieve best results. In this section, we describe these experiments.

Hypotheses

The method is able to correctly validate the given tag assignments to music tracks. The primary target function is the *correctness* i.e. the ratio of correctly evaluated tags to all evaluated tags. Secondary, our goal was to track the *confidence*, i.e. how much of the featured tags the method was confident to evaluate to all tags it featured.

Data

As an input data set, we used the music tag database of the LastFM service (the largest music organization and tagging portal). From it, we took popular 100 music tracks of the pop/rock/rap music domain, 40 top tags (most relevant according to the portal). From these, we cut the top 10 (to remove the best) so we ended up with 3,000 relatively good, but still noisy tags. For the purpose of playback, we used the 7digital music database, from which we used samples lasting from 30 s, to 1 min.

To create a golden standard, each of these tags was evaluated by three independently working experts—people frequently and actively dealing with music, who were asked a dichotomic question, whether the assigned tag to the music is correct or not. The majority vote then determined the validity of the tag.

Participants

The number of players that participated in the experiment was 78. The players were recruited through social networks and email calls. The participation was voluntary and players received no reward. No prior knowledge about the demographics of the participants was considered.

Environment

The game was deployed as a web application. There were no known application accessibility issues.

Process

The game was deployed online for 10 days. During this time 875 games were played (featuring 4,933 questions). Out of the 3,000 tags, 1,492 was used in the game at least once. 17.75 implicit and 5.29 explicit feedback actions were collected averagely for one tag. After the live experiment was closed, the players remained active for several weeks.

During the experiment, the *support* threshold values (ε_{upper}, ε_{lower}) were set to 5 and −5. The parameters ans_c, ans_w and tag_w were handpicked to 0.05, 0.10 and 0.35. After the live experiment was conducted, we run the simulations through combinations of different values of ans_c, ans_w and tag_w (with range between 0 and 1 and the step size 0.1). For each setup, we computed the validity of tags according to game logs and computed the correctness and confidence of the method.

Results

The measurement of *correctness* and *confidence* with the original values of method parameters yielded the following:

- The method was only confident that 487 tags was correctly assigned to their resources (out of 1,492). In 77 % the method was right.
- No tags were marked as wrongly assigned.

Not surprisingly, these results (total confidence 33 % and correctness 77 %) were not good results. Therefore, we proceeded to the simulations where:

- we found a optimal configuration of the parameters $ans_c = 0.2$, $ans_w = 0.3$ and $tag_w = 0.9$.
- Using these parameters, the confidence raised to 51 % with the correctness decreased to 68 %.
- The number of positives (method stated the tag is valid) was still much higher (736) than negatives (method stated the tag is not valid) (39). However, all of these were true negatives, i.e. no correct tag were ruled out by our method.

6.3 Discussion

With CityLights, we demonstrate a game-based method for music tag validation. The design, deployment and experiments with this game have shown us that the method is able to validate the existing music tag sets by harnessing human labor in an engaging game, which maintained its players even after the experiment has ended.

The resulting numbers though, have space for improvement: the method was confident in only one half of the tag cases and reached only 68 % correctness. Fortunately, for the metadata set cleanup scenario, this does not represent a problem. Since the method has zero false negative rate, it does not damage the dataset by removing correct tags. It merely does the job partially: along with the correct tags, it passes some wrong ones too, but those tags would be there anyway if no cleanup is used.

We can also look at the whole problem not as on filtering problem, but as on ranking problem, where task is to re-order the existing tags according to their relevancy (useful for information retrieval methods). For this, the real values of tag *support* from the game could be used directly (after some minimum feedback is collected on the particular tag).

Nevertheless, the results of our method are not completely satisfying and will be subject for future work. The correctness and confidence of the method are moderate. We see several reasons and possible improvements for this:

- Many **tags received not enough feedback** from players to reach any of the two thresholds, lowering the method confidence. These tags may be of two kinds. One is the case of a tag recently introduced to the game. Another case is a tag, the *support* value of which "oscillates" since players see its validity differently. While in the first case, the tag just needs to be featured more in the game, in the second case, the "validation" could go on for long time (or forever), consuming much of the available player "working capacity".
  To distinguish between these two cases, a sort of *support* change momentum (trend) measure could be imposed to detect a "stalemate" situations. Detecting these cases would allow the method to cease featuring of the respective tags and save player work for other. A trend may be defined, for example, as linear approximation of the last n *support* values. In such case, if the trend function is not "steep" enough (either positively or negatively), a "stalemate" situation would be declared for a particular tag. The process may also be two phased. In a first phase, the

algorithm would measure the trend in normal conditions. After a "stalemate" is found, the tag would be featured in the game in "special conditions", meaning that the game would "purposefully" provoke the player to express explicit opinions on this tag. Also the tag could be assigned to "expert players" (see below). In case the stalemate is still present, the featuring of the tag in the game would be ceased. Such approach to sparing of the player work may not necessarily increase correctness of our method, but would certainly improve its output quantity.

- **Lack of player experience in the particular music domain**. In our experiments, we deployed the game limited to certain music genres. Therefore, some players had trouble in recognizing the features of the music and mapping them to tags. Some specific tags imposed problems by themselves: the players (as some of them reported) simply did not understood the tags, as the tags were part of a jargon which the players were not familiar with.

  One solution for this is to let the player to choose genre he is most familiar with (the only issue then is to have enough players for each category). Another is to measure the player competences for individual genres implicitly from his actions in the game (a type of approach we discuss in the second part of this book). With this measure, we can sort the players according to their skill levels for particular music domains and eventually weight the *support* value changes they impose accordingly (assuming that "expert players" give correct feedback more often).

- **"Too dirty dataset"**. It is possible that usability of our method is limited to datasets with only certain range of correct/wrong tag ratio. If for example, the majority of tags within the dataset is wrong, it could cause too much confusion among players, resulting in more biased results. Unfortunately, to determine this, much more experimentation with differently "spoiled" metadata sets must be done.

One more improvement which could help in improving of the output of our method, is taking more of the player behavior into account. What could be considered is the amount of time the player needs or how many times he re-plays the music track to make his decision—possible indicators of hesitation that could be reflected into lower change of the tag *support* value.

References

1. Coviello, E., Chan, A.B., Lanckriet, G.: Time series models for semantic music annotation. Trans. Audio, Speech and Lang. Proc. **19**(5), 1343–1359 (2011)
2. Dittmar, C., Grossmann, H., Cano, E., Grollmisch, S., Lukashevich, H., Abesser, J.: Songs2see and globalmusic2one: two applied research projects in music information retrieval at fraunhofer idmt. In: Proceedings of the 7th International Conference on Exploring Music Contents. CMMR'10, pp. 259–272. Springer-Verlag, Berlin, Heidelberg (2011)
3. Dulačka, P., Šimko, J., Bieliková, M.: Validation of music metadata via game with a purpose. In: Proceedings of the 8th International Conference on Semantic Systems, I-SEMANTICS '12, pp. 177–180. ACM, New York, NY, USA (2012)
4. Miotto, R., Barrington, L., Lanckriet, G.R.G.: Improving auto-tagging by modeling semantic co-occurrences. In: Downie J.S. Veltkamp R.C. (eds.) ISMIR, pp. 297–302. International Society for Music Information Retrieval (2010)

Part II
Designing the Semantics Acquisition Games

Chapter 7
State-of-the-Art: Design of the Semantics Acquisition Games

Abstract This chapter discusses the state-of-the-art of the semantics acquisition games (SAGs) from the perspective of their design, abstracting from their purposes. Our primary concern is the lacking methodology for uneasy SAG creation. At the same time, we are aware of the fact, that even for "regular" games, no such methodology exists. However, we aimed to shed some light on the important design aspects of SAGs by creating a multi-dimensional space representing these aspects. These dimensions focus on issues concerning artifact (game output) validation, task decomposition and difficulty, distribution of tasks (concerning player competences), game aesthetics and motivation, encapsulation of purpose and anti-cheating measures. For each dimension, we have also identified some of their values, which represent various types of SAGs or design patterns used within them.

Today, we observe the use of crowdsourcing games and in particular semantics acquisition games (SAGs) in many problem domains with many individual approaches devised. With growing availability of potential players (i.e. Internet and Web users), the crowdsourcing games will probably gain more prominent place in (and not only in) semantics acquisition field. It can be expected that many new SAG-based solutions will emerge.

Therefore, a relevant question for the future to ask is: how to design them? The SAGs represent a relatively new field (coined first in 2004). While some researchers already aimed to survey the existing SAG approaches [6, 15, 24], only few attempts [22, 28] have been made yet to provide deeper insight on how SAGs should be designed.

The next step for researchers is to try to formulate a holistic theory of SAG design. This is somewhat natural. If we look backward, it also happened to the software design and computer game design: the design theories were formulated only after several programs (resp. games) have been created. In other words, it was possible only after the researchers and practitioners recognized these fields and gathered some experience with it.

We do not have an ambition to formulate a holistic SAG design theory—we merely want to help to explore it. We set up a set of questions, answering which we believe would help understanding the SAG design better. These questions are:

J. Šimko and M. Bieliková, *Semantic Acquisition Games*,
DOI: 10.1007/978-3-319-06115-3_7,

- What mechanisms and rules govern the SAGs? What are their key properties?
- What are the conditions that each SAG must meet to be successful, or to at least have a chance to success?
- Are there any recurring "design patterns" in SAGs?
- What are the good practices in designing the SAGs?
- What are the recurring issues of SAGs that hinder theirs success?
- How can we suppress/mitigate/rule-out these issues?
- Can traditional game design theories and methodologies be useful in designing SAGs?

These questions guide us in our SAG design research. Using them, we examine existing SAG approaches. We identify the design aspects common for all SAGs and issues that SAGs must deal with. We also propose new game mechanisms to solve some of these issues. In all this, we include our own games, which we use to demonstrate our designs.

7.1 Missing Methodology

Designing a SAG is not an easy task. The game must provide entertainment *and* meanwhile harness the human brainpower in a useful way. There is no known argument that would exclude a possible existence of a crowdsourcing game solving *any* computational problem. However, there is also no universal methodology on how to methodically transform an arbitrary *human intelligence task* to a crowdsourcing game. Therefore crowdsourcing games (including SAGs) are currently created ad-hoc. A very ambitious research goal may be the creation of a SAG design methodology, universal or at least suitable for a broader problem-family.

7.1.1 Game Cloning and Casual Playing

Many of the existing SAGs are modified clones of previously existing regular (and popular) games. The motivation? Every game, including SAGs, must attract player's attention in a first place. There are some typical (not necessarily computer) game concepts that are known and widely appreciated by players (secret guessing games, strategies, role playing games, etc.). If a new SAG's scheme is similar to such principles (introducing its purpose by some "trick"), the game has fair potential for appreciation from players. Therefore Vickrey et al. suggested that we should focus on transforming existing games to crowdsourcing games, to maximize their appeal [26].

In connection with that Cusack et al. also stress the notion that computer games should be considered in two groups: classical video games (called also "hardcore"), which are played intensively by narrow group of players and casual games as their opposite (played moderately by many players) [5]. They note that casual games, which emerged in the last decade as web browser games, are gaining more and more players different from players of classical video games: while the typical player of classical video game is a teenage male playing for extensive amount of time a day, the casual games players are of all age categories and of both genders, playing significantly lesser. The potential SAG players recruit from this group, which means that SAGs do not have to compete with elaborated classical video games (which are costly results of years of development), they could be small applications with simple game rules and short play time, to "fill a coffee break time of an mid-aged female office employee".

7.1.2 Von Ahn's Approach

An attempt to formulate a SAG design methodology has been made by von Ahn and Dabbish [28]. Their aim was to come up with an universal abstract scheme for resource description acquisition game, use of which would only depend on the actual resource type. In the game, the player is confronted with a resource and then somehow tricked into directly or indirectly describing it. The authors suggested that a "game with a purpose" should follow one of the three abstract schemes. All of them are two-player schemes (so the players can mutually validate their actions, i.e. the metadata they produce), and use the effect of unconventional socialization and hidden information about the game state (in all schemes, players cooperate, but are unable to communicate with each other).

1. **Output agreement scheme**. In this scheme, the players are given the same resource and then try to blindly agree on a word that describes it. A principle typical for the ESP game [27].
2. **Input agreement scheme**. In this scheme, the players are presented with a resource sample separately. It is either the same for both players or different for each player. After the players see their resource, they describe them and according to this descriptions, the players decide whether they see (hear) the same thing or not. A typical example of this principle is the TagATune game [12].
3. **Inverse problem scheme**. In this scheme, the players have not the same role, instead one is confronted with a resource while other has to guess or correctly select it according to clues created by the first player (which are later mined for metadata). A typical SAG using this scheme is Peekaboom [29]—there the resource is a term which the other player is guessing.

Ahn's ideas have been implemented in many SAGs (his own, but also from other authors). The mechanisms he designed cover a fairly broad group of game purposes in semantics acquisition—mainly involving (multimedia) resource descriptions acquisition. On the other hand, the proposed mechanisms can hardly be used everywhere (e.g. ontology linking, co-reference identification or outside the semantics acquisition, e.g. protein folding or FPGA optimization) and also impose several other problems (e.g. cold start issues) which we cover later. Nevertheless, Ahn and Dabbish left us with a far most "complete" attempt for SAG design methodology?

7.1.3 Mechanics, Dynamics and Aesthetics

If there is an ambition of creating a SAG design methodology, how is it with "common" games design methodologies? One attempt to formulate a formal framework for game design was made by Hunicke et al. and is called *Mechanics Dynamics and Aesthetics* (MDA). It looks at the games from perspectives of three different layers of abstraction [10]:

1. **Aesthetics.** The authors state that the game design should be entertainment driven, and the most abstract layer, the aesthetics describe what emotion would generate the fun (e.g. competition, discovery, self-challenge).
2. **Dynamics.** Contains concepts of how the aesthetics will be realized. It determines what features the game will have (e.g. mercantile system, destruction system, player possessing virtual things, avatar).
3. **Mechanics.** These are the atomic actions of the game that realize the dynamics (shuffling the cards, obstacles on the road, avatar visual properties).

When designing a game, the designer goes simply top–down: he firstly designs the aesthetics level, then dynamics and lastly mechanics. The proposed framework makes sense, but is also very abstract. Its formal model can potentially be used to describe a game, but it cannot guide during the design process in sufficient details.

7.1.4 Design Lenses

Some researchers argue that in classical computer game design or game design in general, there is no existing holistic design methodology yet. Jesse Schell expresses this in his book *The art of game design: the book of lenses* almost anecdotally: there is not even an universally accepted *definition* of a game, how can a methodology for its creation exist then [16]? Accepting that, how can we possibly hope for an SAG design methodology, which would definitely need to satisfy even more requirements than regular game design methodology.

As Schell continues, he tells us that the situation is not that grim. We just do not have an universal recipe for making a game—no "algorithm-like" solution which would make design decisions for us. Mainly because of this, the game design is considered not only as engineering challenge, but also as art.

Instead of a recipe, Schell suggests we should use a set of recommendations for designing a good game, because these we are able to formulate. He proposes a wide set (a hundred) of such recommendations called *lenses*. Each of his lenses focuses on one specific aspect of a game design, stating what conditions should a good game meet in relationship to the given aspect. The lenses test various aspects of the design: the game rules, the relationship with the player, the design process and the designer himself. Practically, this is done by a set of questions that accompany each lens. If a game designer answers these questions sufficiently, his game will *probably* be a good game.

To effectively use the lenses, Schell suggests a strictly iterative, prototype-based approach of the game design and development process, which is inspired by software design and in particular, the agile software design methods. The main iteration scheme is then composed of two parts: first, the designer creates a game prototype and second, he tests the prototype using relevant lenses. Schell stresses that the iterations must be as small as possible and may also run in parallel manner. He also reminds us that iterating includes all of the work on the game design (e.g. artistic work, player analysis), not only the software implementation of the game.

The iterative approach that Schell suggests is a working one—many game designers use its modifications. For us, it is an inspiration. The use of various design dimensions to test the SAG design may be the way to formalize the SAG design process. At least partially. Therefore we focus our research on the identification of SAG design aspects and certain characteristics that SAGs usually share.

7.2 Aspects of SAG Design

Reviewing the design characteristics of existing SAG solutions (including our own) we have identified several design aspects of the semantics acquisition games (note that we consider this list open for the future: we do not claim it is complete):

1. **Validation of player output (semantics and metadata artifacts).** How do SAGs validate if players are creating value when playing? How are the players scored?
2. **Problem decomposition and task difficulty.** Is the problem that SAG solves decomposable into smaller ones? Are all the tasks equally difficult or not? What does it mean for SAG design?
3. **Task distribution and player competences.** Are the competences of all players equal? If not, how does the game distribute the tasks to the players according to their skills?
4. **Player challenges.** This aspect covers the ways the SAG challenges it's players into play. What are the types of game aesthetics that motivate SAG players to play?
5. **Purpose encapsulation.** Is the purpose of the game visible/known to player? How does this influences the player motivation to play?
6. **Cheating vulnerability.** How does the SAG deal with possible security threats and dishonest player behavior?

These aspects serve as a backbone of our classification of SAGs. We introduce them in detail and review the existing SAGs according to them. Each aspect represents one or more requirements a well-functioning SAG must meet. It also represents a set of possible solutions for meeting these requirements. Not always, the solutions are optimal, so we also outline their drawbacks. We later build up on our findings regarding the design aspects and present our own improvements of SAG design, demonstrating it on our games.

7.2.1 Validation of Player Output (Artifacts)

Every SAG has to solve the issue of validation of player output (inferred from the set of actions he does in the game) in order to give him the score feedback. The score must correlate with value of his output from the purpose perspective, otherwise the player would tend to produce outputs with no value in the future. This means the game has to be able to evaluate the value of user output, and has to do it immediately after the game ends, so the player receives feedback and stays motivated to play again.

But how can we evaluate an artifact, which was created by the player for the first time? In other words, if the purpose of the game is to create new artifacts, and creating those artifacts is only within the power of a human, then who, apart from human can validate the correctness of the output?

Many games (like ESP, TagATune and others) [2, 8, 9, 12, 13, 28, 29] rely on *mutual agreement* of two, simultaneously playing players—cooperating or opposing each other (anonymous to each other in case of cooperating players). It's logic is simple, as the players produce artifacts, they are matched together and if they are the same, they are with high probability correct (assuming they have been created independently).

The mutual agreement mechanism however, introduces the *cold-start problem*: there have to be a large enough pool of mutually anonymous players wanting to play at the same time, otherwise, the game cannot even start. This also hinders the desired iterative process of SAG development—it is harder to get a large-enough group of players for testing and user evaluation after every iteration, than to get individual players.

Some SAGs solve this issue by using bot players (based on previous recorded sessions) that validate some of the player's output and provoke him to introduce new facts. A good example of bot use is Vickrey's *Free Association* SAG, where authors claim a relatively large mass of explored metadata relationships (800 thousand term relationship suggestions). This is thanks to the usage of game *bots* which simulated the opposite player in cases when there was only single player wanting to play (this approach was also successfully used by von Ahn in the ESP Game [28]). In fact, almost *all* games were played in "human-bot" mode. Anecdotally, the authors found that most of the players were not even aware that they are playing against a bot [26]— a strong argument to consider possible use of bots in general SAG design.

However (in connection to the cold-start), bots tend to help more in the later stages of SAG deployment. Even if the SAG uses them, it is prone to the cold-start problem in the beginning, where not enough games is pre-recorded. Additionally, use of bots is problem-dependent: not all SAGs can use pre-recorded game sessions, because of a need for inter-player interaction.

Other type of artifact validation approach, which many SAGs rely on, is *bootstrapping*. With bootstrapping, some of the player's output is evaluated according to existing data (according to these, the player gets scored). The rest is taken as new artifacts with high chance of being correct, because player does not know, which of his action (artifact) can and which cannot be evaluated.

Exercising the bootstrapping approach, an interesting framework comprising SAG for image annotation was created by Seneviratne and Izquierdo [17]. It is a single player game. The authors solved the artifact validation issue as follows: as the game input, they mix non-annotated and fully annotated images, transparent to player. At first, the game asks the player to tag the images with existing annotations, then it introduces non-labeled images with an occasional presence of a labeled ones. By tracking the players behavior patterns (using Markov models), the game is able to determine whether the player's behavior is honest or not and determine relevance of the annotations he provided.

Another interesting case of bootstrapping validation model in SAG is the Akinator—the game in which players answer the questions about famous persons and the game "guesses" who it is. The game uses its existing knowledge base to be a solid opponent for a player, while it collect new knowledge as the player answers the questions. If the game "guesses" the correct person at the end, the answers provided by player are used to strengthen that person's attributes in the knowledge base. In case of player's win, the newly introduced character can be immediately provided with some knowledge (answers that the player provided in the game session).

In special cases (depending on the problem being solved), the SAGs are able to validate the player artifacts automatically. We identify two possible forms of automated validation.

The exact automatic validation. In this case, the game is able to exactly compute the value of an artifact according to some metric (e.g. a real fitness value). For example, this is possible when a game solves an NP-Hard problem, where the candidate solutions could be tested with an algorithm with polynomial complexity [5]. Yet, we have observed such scheme only outside the SAG domain, in other crowdsourcing games (e.g. testing the FPGA layout [23] or protein structures [4]).

The approximative automatic validation. In this case, the game is also able to measure the artifact correctness automatically, but with a certain bias, guaranteeing only a partial correlation with the true artifact value. The bias introduces a theoretical risk that the players would be misled to producing wrong artifacts. In practice, the SAGs cover this with not-so-transparent scoring functions, so the players are not able to optimize their solutions to it, or the approximation is simply well enough for the player to stay "on the right track". As typical examples of the approximative artifact validation, we consider our games of Little Search Game and the CityLights. There, a background corpora of not-so-good metadata serves as sources for approximative artifact evaluations. A typical phenomenon, which occur when this model is used, is that the truly valuable artifacts emerge just when the player thinks he was wrong (e.g. the hidden relationships of the LSG or negative feedback on tags in CityLights).

Regardless of the artifact validation model used, each SAG can (and often does) commence a secondary, *after-game* validation: it simply seeks for the consensus between candidate solutions (artifacts) from different game sessions where the same task has been used. This can be done offline, because there is no more need for providing feedback to the player. Using this, any wrong solutions that accidentally passed the primary, *in-game* validation would mostly be filtered. In fact, many SAGs [7, 19, 21, 27, 29] depend heavily on this second step. Nevertheless, we must remember that this secondary validation cannot exist alone within a SAG—each SAG must have some primary artifact validation model implemented.

All of the mentioned (primary) models for artifact validation have several draw-backs (will it be cold start problems, need for data to bootstrap on, or problem dependencies). Therefore, there is a space and need for new models that would over-come these issues. Responding to this, we came up with the *helper artifacts* scheme, which we describe and demonstrate using the PexAce SAG, in Chap. 8.

7.2.2 Problem Decomposition and Task Difficulty

The quantitative potential of SAGs, inherited from crowdsourcing, lies in the massive parallelization of the task being solved, meaning that "a task" is in fact composed of many independent "task instances" which can be assigned to players at will. At the same time, the task instances must be simple enough, so they can be solved in short gameplay sessions. For most currently existing SAGs, the task instances are naturally existing in such a manner: image annotation [9, 27, 29], music annotation [12], term relationship exploration [26]. Note that such SAGs usually use motivation schemes which are *not* based on challenging of the player by task difficulty, because the players would quickly get bored, but by other means (e.g. socialization).

If a SAG aims to solve a bigger problem (e.g. its abstract representation is com-plex), which cannot be solved by a player during a game session, it has to be decom-posable into many sub-tasks. This is a mandatory pre-condition for a SAG: if a big problem cannot be decomposed to lesser problems, then it has a very low chance to be solved by a SAG, because the designer would probably have a problem in making the solving of the problem fun, and there would also be a large "understandability" barrier in acquiring new players to play.

To some extent, a SAG may overcome this problem by introducing a system of gradual increase of difficulty of tasks for a progressing player. After all, it is a common practice of regular games too: over time, the player is confronted with more and more difficult problems. This keeps the player constantly challenged (a positive effect to game's retention) and by solving more complex problems, the player also gains more skill. The best example of a crowdsourcing game implementing this scheme is FoldIt, where players train to create more and more complex proteins [4]. In this particular case, the truly valuable artifacts are created by experienced players only. It is also important to note that the players do not have to possess any special "talent" for the job, they learn how to do it during the game.

The summary from the perspective of problem decomposition and task difficulty is that we have two possible models in SAGs:

1. All tasks are *equal* in their complexity and are relatively easy to solve.
2. There is a gradual increase of complexity of tasks.

7.2.3 Task Distribution and Player Competences

Each SAG operates with a pool of available players and a pool of unsolved (or partially solved tasks). The way how SAGs assign the tasks to the players may greatly influence their outcome, both qualitatively and quantitatively.

First, we might consider the quantitative effectiveness of the game. Let us assume that

1. The SAG requires more than one player to solve a particular task because of the mutual validation, which is needed for majority of problems.
2. There is only limited *available work-power* (i.e. we have a limited number of players with limited average play time). This work-power is lesser than a total *work-power needed* for solving all of the task instances in the pool (i.e. number of all tasks times the number of redundant solutions needed for validation).

If the SAG assigns the tasks to players *randomly* under such conditions, its effectiveness in using the player work will be very small: only a fraction of task instances will be solved sufficient number of times. Therefore, a random scheme is almost never used (the exception might be the games that use exact artifact validation, where no further redundancy in task instance solving is needed once a first correct solution is found). Instead, SAGs apply a *greedy strategy*, which basically pulls those task instances for solving, which are closest to reaching the number of needed solutions. This way, the work (solutions, artifacts) of the players never goes "in vain" as it always participates in the artifact validation.

For the task assignment in SAGs, the greedy strategy can be considered as a baseline. It is usually modified by secondary task-picking criteria, such as:

• Not assigning the same task instance to the same player multiple times (to prevent him to get bored).
• Preferring certain tasks according to some measure of their value (e.g. how important is the resource to be annotated) or to some existing data stubs (e.g. ontology-driven selection [11]).

The approach above optimizes the number of tasks being solved and influences (through the secondary criteria) what tasks are solved with higher priority. On the other hand, it cannot influence the quality of the SAG outcome. The overall "abstract" quality of the SAG output depends on the quality of individual, concrete solutions and these depend on the "quality" of the players they create them (i.e. how good are the solutions of a particular player).

The capabilities (skills, expertise) of individual players are not the same. Some of the players are more suitable to solve certain types of tasks than others. It is therefore suitable to match the players with tasks that best fits their skills. Or to use the knowledge about player expertise to weight his solutions in the process of mutual validation (so the skilled players get more influence than bad players and in the end make the overall SAG output better). The use of "smarter" task assigning in SAGs was firstly proposed by Chiou and Hsu only recently and was yet not followed since [3]. In our work, we conducted our own experiments in applying the knowledge about player expertise.

Summing up, for task distribution, we recognize following design variants, which may also be combined to some extent:

1. Random task selection.
2. Greedy task selection.
3. Task value task selection.
4. Data (ontology) driven task selection.
5. Capability-based player selection.

7.2.4 Player Challenges

Much of the SAG success depends on the motivation for playing it. Primarily, the motivation sources from the entertainment provided by the game: as long as the game entertains the player, he is willing to contribute his time to perform given tasks. Secondarily, we also recognize the (possible) motivation from crowdsourcing point of view: a SAG may appeal to the players also by its purpose (e.g. a contribution to a greater good).

From the game perspective, an important part of the motivation is the type of the pleasure the game offers. Hunicke et al. [10] identified eight types of aesthetics, by which the players of computer games may be entertained. For SAGs, we identify four types (a subset and combination of Hunicke's):

1. Social experience through interaction with other players [1, 25, 28]. The success of online games stands greatly on their social aspects. Online games usually comprise "traditional" features for social interaction (e.g. instant messaging, social network) making them attractive in a similar way as dedicated social web-based applications (e.g. Facebook). Yet these social mechanisms are only side-attached to the actual game mechanism, which are the true benefactors of social interaction. The games truly attract players by unusual rules of interaction, that generate unusual situations, breaking the "real" social context in which the players live. Many SAGs also benefit from the social experience factors defined by game rules. Typically, a recurring human–human interaction-based mechanics within SAGs is "guessing what other player is thinking" resp. on a "hidden truth" about the game state from which every player knows only a part. This combined with limited communication between players, results in intriguing environments.

A significant provision of games with social experience aesthetics is that they are relatively content-independent and are therefore able to sustain the player attention, because players "entertain each other".

2. Competition among players [2, 8, 9, 28]. The competition is traditionally present in many games. For SAGs, we recognize two basic concepts: a *match* between two (or more) players (in which one or more players are victorious) and a *ladder*— a list in which players are sorted according to their scores. While match-based game requires simultaneous participation of multiple players (a danger of cold-start problems), the ladder can be used even when a game session (instance) is occupied by only one player. On the other hand, the ladder-based game bears a risk that many players will loose interest in it because it takes too much effort for the player to reach a position he desires, whereas in the match-based game, the feeling of victory materializes each game.

3. Self-challenge overcoming a player's own previous achievement, joy of reaching a goal [17, 23]. Particularly common for today's SAGs are verbal and visual challenges (involving texts and images). Overcoming these puzzles emulates similar feeling like crossword solving.

4. Discovery—a joy of exploring the game world, e.g. listening to new music in music annotation SAG [1, 12].

Besides game aesthetics classification, we can look at the player's motivation from the crowdsourcing perspective. Various worker incentives are described by literature as usable for crowdsourcing (we list them below). A subset of them is also applicable to SAGs.

1. money (i.e. a monetary or material reward—not applicable to SAGs),
2. goodwill (the participant is satisfied with the good feeling he has upon finishing the work—applicable to SAGs),
3. alignment with personal goals (solving the crowdsourcing task also helps the participant himself—applicable to SAGs, yet not used),
4. fun (a natural part of SAG concept, i.e. the players are attracted by pleasures provided by the game),
5. socialization (corresponds social experience aesthetics found in SAGs) and,
6. reputation and *gamification* (introduction of game aspects and mechanics like leaderboards and badges into an originally non-game working environment— partially covered in SAGs).

The incentives 4, 5 and 6 are somewhat aligned to the previous aesthetics classification. The incentive 1 (money) is relevant to crowdsourcing in general, but exclusive with the SAG principles (which a priori refuse to motivate players by money). The second (goodwill) varies from player to player. The third must be engineered as a part of SAG's design and is currently not used in any existing SAG approach (except our own, presented in this work). Overall, we consider this list as problematic to use for SAG classification, yet it might be useful for a SAG designer, to consider its usage.

One more perspective, from which motivation can be considered is dichotomous: it can be either *external* or *internal* [30]. The internal motivation sources directly from the activity (task solving, game playing). The external motivation is represented by rewards with loose or no connection to the actual activity—they are awarded simply when the job is completed. Such rewards are money, but also reputation points, badges or ranks in ladders. On the other hand, a worker is internally motivated when he participates in the process even without rewards given to him. The motivation in this case may source from goodwill, belief, personal gain (from the activity itself) or, in case of SAGs, fun. In general, the internal motivation is stronger than external—it retains the worker (player) attracted for longer time, but is also harder to achieve.

7.2.5 Purpose Encapsulation

One of the aspects which characterizes a SAG is how apparent (to the player) is its purpose. At one side, a SAG may appear as some kind of work performing interface, not hiding its purpose—the good examples are the image annotation framework of Seneviratne or co-reference identification games with spartan interfaces merely containing the features to perform the purposeful tasks [2, 8, 17]. On the other side, there are SAGs made with substantial efforts to hide (encapsulate) its purpose into other features of the game. A good example of that is the crowdsourcing game Plummings where layout optimization of a city completely covers the underlying FPGA layout optimization task [23]. If we look at the Krause's OnToGalaxy space shooter, we can even observe many features and aesthetics not directly connected to the purpose (e.g. background story, bomb blasts) [11]. Some SAGs are caught between these extremes, for example, in Moodswings [14], where players move a marker in a two dimensional field to express what mood they feel when music plays. The purpose here is somewhat apparent, but everything else makes the game fun and ergonomic, making it easy to forget what purpose the game serves. Naturally, the more the purpose is encapsulated, the less it disturbs the player. However, it comes with a price of additional design and engineering work.

Also, a question a SAG designer has to answer is whether to disclose the purpose of the game to the player or not, i.e. whether to present the game as having a higher purpose or to keep the purpose undeclared. Depending on the context (mostly the player's mindset), this can have two outcomes: at one side the player may loose the interest in the game, because (as Krause et al. warn us) he will start seeing a work in it [11] or refuse to work for someone else for misanthropic reasons. On the other hand, the higher purpose may appeal to the player and convince him to play a game he would otherwise not play (a phenomenon we observed in our own research [20]). Particularly, the player might be convinced, if he too would directly benefit from the purpose (e.g. annotate his own images as in PexAce-Personal [18]). In all cases, regardless if the player knows about the purpose or not, it is convenient if the game encapsulates it.

7.2.6 Cheating and Dishonest Player Behavior

In all computer games, including semantics acquisition games, cheating and dishonest player behavior is a phenomenon that must be considered. Naturally, it is mostly present in the competitive games (in particular with social context), while games based on player self-challenge suffer only a little from this phenomenon. Generally, cheating includes player effort to exploit game rules, various "holes" and bugs or directly interfere with a game's implementation in order to acquire a higher score or some other advantage in a game. This has negative impact on the perception of fairness by other players and may discourage them from playing the game. In case of SAGs, it may also damage the problem solving capability of the game.

Semantics acquisition games usually deal with the threat of dishonest player behavior by pursuing *restrictive rules* to discourage players from cheating (e.g. preventive banning of certain tags from use [20]) or they have control mechanisms based on *mutual player supervision* [9, 28]. An example is the ESP game where dishonest player behavior is a considerable issue. The possible situation of such case is when players somehow agree on certain words (e.g. via some obscure portal), which they enter as tags for each image. The ESP Game solves this issue by various heuristics (e.g. tracking the recurrence of certain words, identifying typical "cheating" behavior patterns) [28]. In KissKissBan game, Ho et al. added to this by mutual player supervision introduced by new player—opponent to the two collaborating players.

Some SAGs even analyze the player's behavior on-the-fly: the SAG Akinator (popular person guessing and information harvester) is able to detect random question answering of the player (and discourage them from such further behavior by taunting the player). The Seneviratne's framework combines the machine learning for dishonest behavior with checking the artifacts against a validation data set [17].

In our research, we introduce an *a posteriori anti-cheating heuristics* for SAGs, based on the notion that for solving human intelligence tasks, it is unlikely that an automated cheating method would produce them in sufficient quality (if so, there would be no need for the game). Therefore, player actions earning highest scores in the game can always be examined whether they lead to the creation of useful artifacts. If not, they may be subject to disqualification.

To sum up, SAGs implement the following anti-cheating strategies (including combinations):

1. Prevention by restrictive rules.
2. Mutual player supervision.
3. Anomalous behavior pattern detection (machine learning, validation data use).
4. A posteriori cheating detection.

7.3 Evaluation of SAGs: Attention, Retention and Throughput

A SAG designer may consider a formal measurement of the effectiveness of his game. In evaluating general game, two aspects are usually measured:

1. **Attraction**, or a number of players (per unit of time) the game is able to attract to play for trial. The game must be appealing for the player from the very first experience with it. If it is not, though it may even be the best game ever created in it's later stages, it will never attract the player to play it and it therefore reduces it's own potential. This happens for instance when the game rules are complex and the player firstly need to understand them to start playing, which most players refuse to do.
2. **Retention**, or how long (averagely) the players remain attracted to the game and return to it for more playing. A game might entertain the player for only limited amount of time and after that, the player ceases to play it. From this point of view, the games based on social experience of the players have more potential than self-challenge (which is exceed when player reaches his limits) and competition-based games (which may lead to the player's frustration that he is not the winner). Of course, this depends on the prevailing characteristics of target player groups (e.g. males are more responsive to competition while females to socialization [16]).

Multiplication of these two measures results in the total number of man-hours that players spent playing the game and a natural goal of game designers is to increase this factor as much as possible.

The semantics acquisition games have the very same goal. Their effectiveness is however, determined by more factors, namely:

1. **Game throughput** or how many task instances (in average) is a player able to solve within 1 h of playing (this measure was introduced by von Ahn [28] who complemented it with average lifetime play, which corresponds to our retention).
2. **Average quality of solutions delivered**. This complements the previous quantitative factor. For some tasks, the quality of valid artifacts is the is irrelevant, for example an information, whether an image contains human figure or not cannot have multiple levels of quality. On the other hand, we can define a quality measure correlated, for example, to tag specificness in a game that deliver image tags.

7.4 SAG Design at a Glance: Discussion

We see that the field of design of semantics acquisition games comprises several design perspectives, from which we can look at them. We have identified and described six of them (they are summarized in a virtual six-dimensional space in the Fig. 7.1). Each dimension represents a particular design issue which each SAG has to overcome and is accompanied with several solution types or "design patterns" used

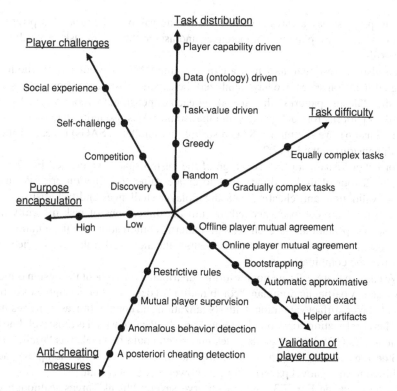

Fig. 7.1 Six design dimensions of semantics acquisition games. Each axis represents one design dimension. The values on the axes represent different types of solutions (design patterns) that SAGs feature to solve issues that dimensions represent. SAGs sometimes use more than one types of solutions

as standards by SAGs. Almost each SAG (when differences in purposes are counted) represents an unique combination of the design patterns and features. Overall the "design space" represents a system of trade-offs that balance the amount technical, artistic and marketing work of designers at one side and cold start problems, vulnerability to malicious player behavior, attraction, retention and game output quality and quantity on the other side.

Some of the design dimensions represent critical problems which must be overcame by each SAG (using one of the patterns), other merely adjust the final output of the game. As critical, we could consider *validation of player output* (which must be done in order to properly score the player), the *anti-cheating measures* (which must deal with all threats the game rules impose) and *player challenges* (from which at least one must be present in the game). Satisfaction of these is a requirement for a successful SAG. On the other hand, using a random *task distribution* or low *purpose encapsulation*, won't necessarily disable the whole game concept, but may seriously decrease the quality and quantity of game's output. At the same time, the existing SAGs can always be polished along these dimensions (e.g. SAG randomly assigning tasks to players may always start to measure the value of the tasks and prioritize them or to measure players' competences and assign them with tasks according to their skills).

It is also interesting to look how are the existing SAGs distributed throughout the design dimension space: we have analyzed the existing SAG-based approaches and identified "design patterns" they use along each dimension. In Table 7.1 we list the identified patterns for each game (note that some SAGs use more than one pattern per dimension). We summarize SAG distribution (number of SAGs) for each pattern (per dimension) in the Fig. 7.2.

For better visualization of coverage of the design space, we created Fig. 7.3. In it we used four of the six dimensions to create value combination grid. We used artifact validation, anti-cheating measures, player challenges and task distribution. To keep the table compact, needed to omit the dimensions of task difficulty and purpose encapsulation. For each "design pattern" combination, we list a number of SAGs using it. We colored the table segments—the more darker the area is, the more repetitive the combination is.

We can see that SAGs are not uniformly distributed throughout the design dimension space. A particular dominant "combination" of design patterns comprises online mutual player artifact validation, with socialization and competition as game aesthetics. This combination corresponds to von Ahn's ESP game which is most well known and many SAGs follow its general design, which could be labeled as "traditional" SAG design. In the future, the relative weight (in terms of existing examples) could be shifted to more novel patterns, for this however, we must wait.

Throughout the Fig. 7.3, we can observe several "blank" areas. Although the matrix is sparse, there are whole sections not covered by existing SAG solutions. The question is, whether these blank spaces will be covered by some solutions in the future. First, we considered two "primary" dimensions, artifact validation and player challenges:

- The SAGs which are based on social experience aesthetics exercise online mutual validation of artifacts. This is connected to the multiplayer nature of these games: a social experience is hardly achievable without multiplayer scheme. So if we already have a multiplayer SAG, it is natural to use online mutual validation of artifacts. Use of other validation schemes here is possible for these games, but is more likely considered redundant.

- On the other hand, the competition aesthetics that is used heavily within existing SAGs is not exclusive for online mutual artifact validation. This is because of the use of "offline" motivation features, such as ladders, which are available for all types of games. However, it is questionable how effective this incentive is in single-player games as the ladder can be considered as external motivation feature. In the future, the SAGs in this setting will perhaps adopt the concept of endogenous value (described by Schell [16]), which means they will enable players to re-use their acquired ladder positions (or points, badges, etc.) in the game itself. This would give an additional meaning for the external incentives and perhaps prolong an average lifetime of the SAG.

Table 7.1 Summary of features used in existing SAGs according to design dimensions

Game	Artifact validation	Task difficulty	Task distribution	Challenges	Purpose encaps.	Anti-cheating measures
Text description						
Phrase detec.	Online mutual	Equal	Greedy, task value	Competition	Low	N/A
PlayCoref	Online mutual	Equal	Greedy, task value	Competition	Low	Rules
Image description						
ESP	Online mutual	Equal	Greedy, task value	Socializ., comp.	Medium	Anom., rules
KissKissBan	Online mutual	Equal	Greedy, task value	Socializ., comp.	Medium	An., r., mut.
Peekaboom	Online mutual	Equal	Greedy, task value	Socializ., comp.	High	Rules
(Seneviratne)	Bootstrapping	Equal	Greedy, task value	Comp.	Low	Anom.
PexAce	Helper artifacts	Equal	Greedy, TV, capab.	Comp., disc., self.	Low	Aposteriori, rules
(Chiou)	Online mutual	Equal	Capability–based	Socializ., comp.	Medium	Anom., rules
Audio description						
TagATune	Online mutual	Equal	Greedy, task value	Socializ., comp.	Medium	N/A
(Mandel)	Bootstrapping	Equal	Greedy, task value	Competition	Medium	Rules
Listen game	Online mutual	Equal	Greedy, task value	Socializ., comp.	Medium	N/A
Herdlt	Online mutual	Equal	Greedy, task value	Socializ., comp.	Medium	N/A
Moodswings	Online mutual	Equal	Greedy, task value	Socializ., comp.	Medium	N/A
CityLights	Aut. approx.	Gradual	Greedy	Comp., disc., self.	Medium	Rules
Atomic fact collectors						
Verbosity	Online mutual	Equal	Greedy, task value	Socializ., comp.	Medium	Rules
GuessWhat!?	Online mutual	Gradual	Data-driven	Socializ., comp.	Low	Mutual
Categorilla	Online mutual	Equal	Greedy	Socializ., comp.	Low	Anom., rules

(continued)

Table 7.1 (continued)

Game	Artifact validation	Task difficulty	Task distribution	Challenges	Purpose encaps.	Anti-cheating measures
Categodzilla	Online mutual	Equal	Greedy	Socializ., comp.	Low	Anom., rules
FreeAsso.	Online mutual	Equal	Greedy	Socializ., comp.	Medium	Anom., rules
LSG	Aut. approx.	Equal	Greedy, data-driven	Comp., self.	Low	Anom., rules
Ontology expansion						
OnToGalaxy	Bootstrapping	Equal	Data-driven	Self.	High	N/A
OntoPronto	Online mutual	Equal	Data-driven	Socializ., comp.	Low	Anom., rules
OntoTube	Online mutual	Equal	Greedy	Socializ., comp.	Low	Anom., rules
OntoBay	Online mutual	Equal	Greedy	Socializ., comp.	Low	Anom., rules
Akinator	Bootstrapping	Equal	Data-driven	Self.	High	Anom.
Ontology connecting						
SpotTheLink	Online mutual	Equal	Data-driven	Socializ., comp.	Low	Anom., rules
Misc						
Plummings	Aut. exact	Gradual	Task-value	Self., comp.	High	Anom.
FoldIt	Aut. exact	Gradual	Task-value	Self., comp.	High	Anom.

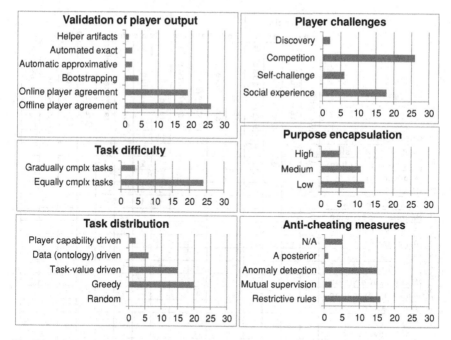

Fig. 7.2 SAG design dimensions—number of SAGs per each pattern

- The Fig. 7.3 shows us that discovery as a game aesthetics is used only sparsely for SAGs. Yet, we were quite strict in associating of this "pattern" to SAGs: we only counted SAGs, authors of which explicitly "declare" they entertain players by their content (in fact, these were only our PexAce and CityLights). However, if we admit that, for example, all "multimedia-related" SAGs to some extent entertain players by new multimedia content, the discovery columns of the table would be more populous. It may be viable for the future development of multimedia metadata acquisition games, to consider relying more on the discovery aesthetics, by adaptive selection of content potentially attractive to players.

As can be seen in the Fig. 7.3, the two "secondary" dimensions (anti-cheating measures and task distribution) further concretize the allocation of existing SAGs. We can, for example, we may observe a relatively low utilization of mutual player supervision (as anti-cheating measure) in multiplayer (online player agreement) games. This is because these games are in majority cooperative, not competitive on the session level. On the other hand, other anti-cheating measures such as restrictive rules and anomaly detection are used with all types of games. Considering the task distribution, there is a overall dominance of greedy approach (as this is natural and easy to implement) seconded by task-value driven approaches, followed by data- and player capability-driven approaches. Yet, no apparent differences in SAG counts can be observed regarding other dimensions. The only one we noticed, was a slightly higher use of data-driven task assignment for single player games.

		Social experience				Self-challenge				Competition				Discovery			
		Greedy	Task-value	Data-driven	Player capability	Greedy	Task-value	Data-driven	Player capability	Greedy	Task-value	Data-driven	Player capability	Greedy	Task-value	Data-driven	Player capability
O. mutual	Restrictive rules	9	4	2	1					10	5	2	1				
	Mutual supervision	1	1	1						1	1	1					
	Anomaly detection	7	2	2	1					7	2	2	1				
	A posteriori																
	N/A	4	4							5	5						
Bootstrap.	Restrictive rules									1	1						
	Mutual supervision																
	Anomaly detection							1		1	1						
	A posteriori																
	N/A									1							
Aut. Approx	Restrictive rules					2		1		2		1		1			
	Mutual supervision																
	Anomaly detection					1		1		1		1					
	A posteriori																
	N/A																
Aut. Exact	Restrictive rules																
	Mutual supervision																
	Anomaly detection							2				2					
	A posteriori																
	N/A																
Helper art.	Restrictive rules									1	1		1	1	1		1
	Mutual supervision																
	Anomaly detection																
	A posteriori									1	1		1	1	1		1
	N/A																

Fig. 7.3 Coverage of SAG "design space" by individual SAGs. The more populous combinations are colored *darker*

One more interesting distribution of patterns we found the purpose encapsulation. Some games, especially those that require typing or working with texts disclose their purpose more obviously (having low purpose encapsulation). For multimedia description SAGs, the music description games perform relatively better. Best results in encapsulating however, are characteristic for games with unique game mechanics or games where designers spent much more time polishing the game aesthetics.

What does the SAG experience mean to the general crowdsourcing? Could some of SAG ideas be useful for other types of crowdsourcing approaches? Some of the SAG issues (design dimensions) are common for crowdsourcing field (more or less, SAGs inherit these issues from crowdsourcing). These include:

- **Malicious behavior detection**. Just as for SAGs, it is equally important for "conventional" crowdsourcing approaches like Mechanical Turk where micro-payments for solving tasks are imposed. Here, practitioners must always fight spammers, who attempt to pull out micro payments for fake task solutions.

- **Task distribution regarding worker competences**. The idea is the same as with SAGs. In order to achieve best output, a task should be assigned to worker most competent for it.

The crowdsourcing approaches have their own methods on dealing with these issues, some very similar to methods found in SAGs. For example, for spam detection, crowdsourcing platforms implement machine learned pattern recognition that mine worker behavior logs to find spammer-characteristic patterns, which is analogous to the anomaly detection imposed by some SAGs. Some methods utilized by SAGs however, are not common in crowdsourcing, for example a mutual worker supervision during a simultaneous task solving analogous to the mutual player supervision. The crowdsourcing may still get inspired.

The SAGs experience also shows us that people can be engaged for useful activity through playing. The only downside is, that it is really hard to make this work for an arbitrary problem. Some research an practitioners are therefore turning to a more "lightweight" approach and try to introduce playful experience into existing working processes (instead of inventing games into which work is incorporated) (i.e. gamification).

References

1. Barrington, L., O'Malley, D., Turnbull, D., Lanckriet, G.: User-centered design of a social game to tag music. In: Proceedings of the ACM SIGKDD Workshop on Human Computation, HCOMP '09, pp. 7–10. ACM, New York (2009)
2. Chamberlain, J., Poesio, M., Kruschwitz, U.: A demonstration of human computation using the phrase detectives annotation game. In: Proceedings of the ACM SIGKDD Workshop on Human Computation, HCOMP '09, pp. 23–24. ACM, New York (2009)
3. Chiou, C.L., Hsu, J.Y.J.: Capability-aligned matching: improving quality of games with a purpose. In: The 10th International Conference on Autonomous Agents and Multiagent Systems AAMAS '11, vol. 2, pp. 643–650. International Foundation for Autonomous Agents and Multiagent Systems, Richland (2011)
4. Cooper, S., Treuille, A., Barbero, J., Leaver-Fay, A., Tuite, K., Khatib, F., Snyder, A.C., Beenen, M., Salesin, D., Baker, D., Popović, Z.: The challenge of designing scientific discovery games. In: Proceedings of the Fifth International Conference on the Foundations of Digital Games, FDG '10, pp. 40–47. ACM, New York (2010)
5. Cusack, C., Martens, C., Mutreja, P.: Volunteer computing using casual games. In: Proceedings of Future Play 2006 International Conference on the Future of Game Design and Technology, pp. 1–8. Citeseer (2006)
6. Das, R., Vukovic, M.: Emerging theories and models of human computation systems: a brief survey. In: Proceedings of the 2nd international Workshop on Ubiquitous crowdsouring, Ubi-Crowd '11, pp. 1–4. ACM, New York (2011)
7. Dulačka, P., Šimko, J., Bieliková, M.: Validation of music metadata via game with a purpose. In: Proceedings of the 8th International Conference on Semantic Systems, I-SEMANTICS '12, pp. 177–180. ACM, New York (2012)

8. Hladka, B., Mirovsky, J., Schlesinger, P.: Designing a language game for collecting coreference annotation. In: Proceedings of the Third Linguistic Annotation Workshop, pp. 52–55. Association for Computational Linguistics (2009)

9. Ho, C.J., Chang, T.H., Lee, J.C., Hsu, J.Y.j., Chen, K.T.: Kisskissban: a competitive human computation game for image annotation. In: Proceedings of the ACM SIGKDD Workshop on Human Computation, HCOMP '09, pp. 11–14. ACM, New York (2009)

10. Hunicke, R., Leblanc, M., Zubek, R.: Mda: a formal approach to game design and game research. In: In Proceedings of the Challenges in Games AI Workshop Nineteenth National Conference of Artificial Intelligence, pp. 1–5. Press (2004)

11. Krause, M., Takhtamysheva, A., Wittstock, M., Malaka, R.: Frontiers of a paradigm: exploring human computation with digital games. In: Proceedings of the ACM SIGKDD Workshop on Human Computation, HCOMP '10, pp. 22–25. ACM, New York (2010)

12. Law, E.L.M., Von Ahn, L., Dannenberg, R.B., Crawford, M.: Tagatune: a game for music and sound annotation. In: International Conference on Music, Information Retrieval (ISMIR'07), pp. 361–364 (2007)

13. Markotschi, T., Völker, J.: GuessWhat?! human intelligence for mining linked data. In: Proceedings of the Workshop on Knowledge Injection into and Extraction from Linked Data (KIELD) at the International Conference on Knowledge Engineering and Knowledge Management (EKAW) pp. 1–12 (2010)

14. Morton, B.G., Speck, J.A., Schmidt, E.M., Kim, Y.E.: Improving music emotion labeling using human computation. In: Proceedings of the ACM SIGKDD Workshop on Human Computation, HCOMP '10, pp. 45–48. ACM, New York (2010)

15. Quinn, A.J., Bederson, B.B.: Human computation: a survey and taxonomy of a growing field. In: Proceedings of the SIGCHI Conference on Human Factors in Computing Systems. CHI '11, pp. 1403–1412. ACM, New York (2011)

16. Schell, J.: The Art of Game Design a Book of Lenses, 1 edn. Elsevier/Morgan Kaufmann, Massachusetts (2008)

17. Seneviratne, L., Izquierdo, E.: An interactive framework for image annotation through gaming. In: Proceedings of the International Conference on Multimedia Information Retrieval, MIR '10, pp. 517–526. ACM, New York (2010)

18. Šimko, J., Bieliková, M.: Personal image tagging: a game-based approach. In: Proceedings of the 8th International Conference on Semantic Systems, I-SEMANTICS '12, pp. 88–93. ACM, New York (2012). doi:10.1145/2362499.2362512

19. Šimko, J., Tvarožek, M., Bieliková, M.: Little search game: term network acquisition via a human computation game. In: Proceedings of the 22nd ACM Conference on Hypertext and hypermedia, HT '11, pp. 57–62. ACM, New York (2011)

20. Šimko, J., Tvarožek, M., Bieliková, M.: Semantics discovery via human computation games. Int. J. Semantic Web Inf. Syst. 7(3), 23–45 (2011)

21. Šimko, J., Tvarožek, M., Bieliková, M.: Human computation: image metadata acquisition based on a single-player annotation game. Int. J. Hum. Comput. Stud. 71(10), 933–945 (2013)

22. Syu, Y.S., Yu, H.H., Chen, L.J.: Exploiting puzzle diversity in puzzle selection for esp-like gwap systems. In: Proceedings of the 2010 IEEE/WIC/ACM International Conference on Web Intelligence and Intelligent Agent Technology, WI-IAT '10, vol. 01, pp. 468–475. IEEE Computer Society, Washington (2010)

23. Terry, L., Roitch, V., Tufail, S., Singh, K., Taraq, O., Luk, W., Jamieson, P.: Harnessing human computation cycles for the fpga placement problem. In: Plaks, T.P. (ed.) ERSA, pp. 188–194. CSREA Press, Las Vegas (2009)

24. Thaler, S., Siorpaes, K., Simperl, E., Hofer, C.: A survey on games for knowledge acquisition. Technical report, Semantic Technologies Institute, University of Innsbruck (2011)

25. Tuulos, V.H., Scheible, J., Ojala, T.: Story mashup: design and evaluation of novel interactive storytelling game for mobile and web users. In: Proceedings of the 6th International Conference on Mobile and Ubiquitous Multimedia, MUM '07, pp. 139–148. ACM, New York (2007)

26. Vickrey, D., Bronzan, A., Choi, W., Kumar, A., Turner-Maier, J., Wang, A., Koller, D.: Online word games for semantic data collection. In: Proceedings of the Conference on Empirical Methods in Natural Language Processing, EMNLP '08, pp. 533–542. Association for Computational Linguistics, Morristown (2008)

27. von Ahn, L., Dabbish, L.: Labeling images with a computer game. In: Proceedings of the SIGCHI Conference on Human Factors in Computing Systems, CHI '04, pp. 319–326. ACM, New York (2004)

28. von Ahn, L., Dabbish, L.: Designing games with a purpose. Commun. ACM **51**(8), 58–67 (2008)

29. von Ahn, L., Liu, R., Blum, M.: Peekaboom: a game for locating objects in images. In: Proceedings of the SIGCHI Conference on Human Factors in Computing Systems, CHI '06, pp. 55–64. ACM, New York (2006)

30. Zichermann, G., Cunningham, C.: Gamification by Design: Implementing Game Mechanics in Web and Mobile Apps. O'Reilly, Media (2011)

Chapter 8
Our SAGs: Design Aspects and Improvements

Abstract We follow up with our semantics acquisition game (SAG) design classification, presented in previous chapter. In this chapter, we focus on our own contributions to this design space—new "design patterns". We demonstrate them on our semantics acquisition games: the Little Search Game, PexAce and CityLights. The contributions include novel "helper artifact" validation scheme helping to overcome cold-start problems of SAGs, anti-cheating measures usable in SAGs, concept of a "validation SAG" (used for validation of existing artifacts rather than creation of new ones) and approaches for measuring player competences in SAGs (and applying them to improve game outcomes).

We introduced the SAG design aspects in the previous chapter and reviewed the existing SAGs from the design perspective. Now we review our own SAG solutions from their design point of view. We also present our contributions to the SAG design field—design features of our SAGs that can be generalized and used elsewhere.

Apart from the purposes which we wanted to fulfill, our a priori design requirement (and a unifying feature) for all of our SAGs was to make them single-player, but still capable to properly feedback on player's efforts. Everything, to overcome the cold-start problems most of the SAGs have. Each of our games dealt with this assignment differently, exercises various mechanisms of artifact validation and various forms of player motivation to play. We also had to consider anti-cheating measures for some games. Moreover, we implemented mechanisms exploiting the variances in the player individual skills.

8.1 Little Search Game

From a SAG design standpoint, the *Little Search Game* [5] (as well as its modification *Term Blaster*) is a single-player game where players are engaged in a ladder-based competition. It requires no large set of input data except few task words. Therefore, it has no cold-start issue to be solved, it can be played anytime.

J. Šimko and M. Bieliková, *Semantic Acquisition Games*,
DOI: 10.1007/978-3-319-06115-3_8,
© Springer International Publishing Switzerland 2014

Concerning *artifact validation method*, the game exercises an approximative automated validation combined with the offline mutual agreement. Here, the "approximative" means that the winning conditions of the game is not equal with desired artifacts we want to acquire from the game (i.e. the hidden term relationship), they are only aligned through the scheme of the score computation: the player receives points only when he effectively reduces the search result set with some negative terms—but those negative terms are not necessarily related to the given task term, nor the terms related to the task term always yield decrease of the number of returned results. However, player probably achieves best score, if he tries out some truly task-term related negative terms, which reduces the number of cases when players tend to play without following the game's purpose.

Regarding *problem decomposition*, the game's purpose (of exploring term relationships) is naturally composed of many small tasks (terms to be attached with relationships), therefore, we found to trouble in an eventual problem decomposition. The *tasks can also be considered equal* in their difficulty if we consider them within a single domain: although the individual players may find different task terms not equally difficult, no systematic difficulty differences could be considered without some external knowledge about the task terms (to eventually form a gradual difficulty mode of the game). Of course, the difficulty differences between the tasks can be expected *between the domains* for which the term relationships are collected: the player performing well within a general domain may completely fail in some specific domain.

8.1.1 Player Motivation, Ladder System

In *Little Search Game* (LSG) some of the attractiveness is motivated by the element of *challenge* (i.e., by the opportunity to outdo oneself), which is represented by a mental challenge for players to come up with negative terms which really help them. The second part of attractiveness is *competition*. The challenge aspect is always present in the game, even if the player plays it alone. On the other hand, the competition depends on the comparison with the other players through the ladder system.

For LSG, the ladder is in fact the critical point where our attractiveness and throughput requirements initially contradicted which caused design complications.

Unfortunately, the desired competition aesthetics (fueled by comparison through score and ladder) contradicted the requirements on game's throughput. A fair competition in Little Search Game requires that the players play with the same task terms, so their scores (sourcing from search result count decreases) could be directly compared. This, however, results into only few task terms, over which the may players play. In addition, players naturally tended to make many attempts over lesser numbers of task terms (they tried to refine their negative search terms). As a result, many term relationships would be created, but with only few source terms (dense and small network). And our desire was the opposite: we aimed to create a sparser network with more source terms (concretely, we opted for 10 relationships per term, since we originally aimed to use the network visualized in exploratory search tasks). For this, we needed only limited number of players playing the game with a same task term. We have to come up with a task assigning strategy that would not break the direct competition between players.

The answer is to organize the gameplay within "ladder periods" lasting from several days to several week (the exact duration depends on the number of players participating). Each period has a set of task terms assigned to it—the players are able to play only with them during the period. At the start of the period, the ladders are reset, so the competition begin anew. This, as a side effect, aimed at attracting new players to the game.

To prevent the players from playing with just one task term (which is possible, since it is within player's power to repeat as many attempts as he wants), the game keeps a separate *task ladder* for each term and then a *joint* ("overall") ladder. The arithmetic of the joint ladder simply accumulate the partial results found in task ladders: for each task ladder the player has a rank in (i.e. he has finished at least one game with that particular term), he receives points to the joint ladder, based on his relative position within that task ladder. The set of terms for one period is relatively small (up to ten terms), so it is within reason to play with them all for a regular player and have a chance to reach the maximum score in the joint ladder (which is, naturally, the most prestigious one).

8.1.2 Cheating Vulnerability and a Posteriori Cheating Detection

After the initial design of the Little Search Game and its first deployment, it was soon apparent that the game is prone to two types of unfair or malicious player behavior:

1. **The use of stopwords**. The LSG scores players according to real web co-occurrence of terms. Guessing semantically related words to a given task word is a fair challenge and is encouraged by the game. Unfortunately, there is a workaround: the player may easily use some very frequently used words instead and achieve even "better results" (lower number-of-result yield), while providing absolutely no value to the purpose of the game and possibly ruining the game's competition. Such frequent words may be stopwords of the language (e.g. prepositions), corpus (e.g. "software" in a specific domain of software engineering) or syntactic features of the corpus resources (e.g. HTML tags indexed by the search engine, such as "table", or words frequently used for structuring the websites, such as "menu").

2. **Interfering with game implementation**. This is a rather "standard" threat of many regular games, particularly online, competitive games. An interfering with game's network communication between the client and server is the usual type of attack. A standard solution to this is executing all of the game's logic to the server, leaving the client with mere visualization and interaction functions (i.e. the set of actions available to the player is equivalent with set of actions available

through game's server API). In our case, we could not do the entire game logic at our server, because we were dependent on the external search engines, whose API we could not queried from one (server) machine (because of queries-per-day limits) but from multiple client machines. Therefore, the client side told our server about the search result count and this opened the possibility to spoof the communication to our server (resp. the communication from the search engine to our clients) and provide false results. Since we have not very wide audience for the game, we experienced this type of attack only once. Nevertheless, we have to take some measures that ultimately led us to the creation of the a posteriori cheating detection.

Concerning the Term Blaster modification of the LSG, the stopword threat was solved by the game mechanics, the set of words allowed to use was defined by the game itself. The game danger of interfering with the game's implementation was also ruled-out: the search engine was now part of the game's implementation on the server side and thus, we were able to handle all of the logic in the safe environment with no options for "result spoofing".

8.1.2.1 Term Banning

The "stopword deviation" is a downside effect of the approximative artifact validation method. It comes with the probability that player realizes the possibility of exploiting the scoring rules. In this case, the scoring mechanism was simple and known to the players, so some of them realized the possibility of using a stopword as a "ultimate word". Technically, by entering stopwords, player is not violating the game rules, but due to it's negative effects, we needed to restrict this.

We restricted the stopwords by explicitly banning them (*prevention by restrictive rules*). We did so by imposing several rules:

- All negative search terms used by players must be contained within a dictionary (we used WordNet) as either nouns, adjectives, verbs or adverbs (this effectively excludes most words that carry no semantics, though as a downside it also prevents usage of perfectly valid terms outside of the dictionary).
- The player cannot use the same term as within the task query (including its morphs, checked by a dictionary).
- The most frequent words of the language cannot be used. We used 200 most frequent English words from Wikipedia.
- The player cannot use words, which are commonly acting as HTML tags or which are commonly used for creating website structure (e.g. "menu"). We have prepared this set manually.

When players attempted to use these, they received a message explaining why they cannot do so. The ban-list initially helped during the gameplay, and kept many players from experimenting with stopwords. However, some still continued in finding words working like stopwords which were at the same time not yet banned. To identify these, we initially manually reviewed the use of terms in the game and later let a posteriori cheating detection heuristics (described below) to identify them for us. Over time, the ban list grew and became an effective tool for preventing the abuse of stopwords.

Unfortunately, some terms had to be excluded from the game (and thus the resulting term network) even though they arguably had semantic meaning and legitimacy to be used as negative terms in certain tasks (e.g., "restaurant -menu" or "school -table", where "menu" and "table" are banned due to being common in web content and HTML code). Such terms had to be sacrificed in order to keep the game fair; though they could still be used as task words.

8.1.2.2 A Posteriori Cheating Detection

Regarding the second type of threat—the hacking of the game's implementation—no prevention rules were possible. While this was a problem-dependent issue, it led us to a cheating detection scheme which is generalizable to other semantics acquisition games.

Our *a posteriori cheating detection heuristics* suggests suspicious players and potential stopwords to game administrators. The premise is that *suspicious player actions* (such is the use of stopwords)

1. would result in high ladder rankings of the cheaters,
2. would result in repetition of a same player behavior for different tasks and
3. would result to marginal contributions to the usefulness of the game's output.

The more these conditions are satisfied for one player, the more is this player suspicious for performing "unwanted actions". For the Little Search Game, the heuristics works following these steps:

1. Collect highest ranking players (their number is parametric).
2. Collect their best attempts (sets of negative search terms) for tasks where they ranked high.
3. Drop terms appearing in only one task.
4. Mark "suspicious" terms, i.e. terms that significantly decreased the number of results for more than one task term. Pass them to administrator.

For each of the suspicious terms, two measures are computed to aid the administrator in deciding whether to ban the term (or the player that used it) or not. The first measure is universal for any SAG, the second is problem dependent—related only to the LSG:

1. The consensus participation (interval between 0 and 1). How many players agree on this term for this task (relative to other terms players agree on)? If the suspicious term (artifact in general) is used by other players too for the same task, it is likely not abusive.

2. Stopword probability (interval between 0 and 1). The method queries the suspicious term for the average co-occurrence with a set of 10 manually selected reference terms (with a small mutual co-occurrence on Web). Alternatively, the document frequency of the term can be used. If the co-occurrence with them is high, the terms are more likely to be stopwords.

It is then up to the game administrator to judge, whether the term should be banned. However, these measures allows a quick filtering of the candidates.

During the game deployment, the number of banned terms increased from 230 to 430. The "a posteriori" heuristics was able to identify 30 terms not suitable for the game. The rest of the banned terms was inferred by game administrator according to these 30 terms. For example, in one case, the suggested problematic term was a number (unfortunately, present in a dictionary). This naturally led the administrator to also ban other numbers.

8.1.2.3 A Posteriori Cheating Detection: A Generalization

Based on what we described above, we formulate the general a posteriori cheating detection method for semantics acquisition games. It is a regression based anomaly detection. It consist of the following steps:

1. Collect player produced problem solutions (artifacts).
2. Assign these artifacts with score the players received for creating them.
3. Measure the "usefulness" of the solution. This is problem-dependent, in all cases however, the "usefulness" can be substituted by measuring the participation of each solution on the consensus (*consensus rates*), i.e. how large is the support of players for this solution in comparison to the solution which is supported most?
4. Create a relation of between usefulness (x-axis) and the score (y-axis). Compute its regression of an order considered optimal (e.g. linear, if the players are meant to be rewarded linear to the value they provide).
5. Identify outliers above the regression (high scores), these are the suspicious solutions.

Instead of artifacts themselves, the *behavioral patterns* (of the players) that led to the artifacts may also be considered. The behavioral pattern is an abstract sequence of player's actions that somehow characterize player's behavior in the game (for example, typing and deleting the same word repeatedly). It might be viable if the game mechanics are not so simple and may be combined in many ways to create problem solutions. If for example, a pattern has led to a suspicious solution, it may be a good idea to investigate where else this pattern occurred.

8.1.3 Evaluating the Appeal to the Player

We also conducted series of experiments to examine how players perceive the Little Search Game in terms of attractiveness [4, 5], which is one of two key factors in quantifying the SAG impact [6] (the second one is *throughput*, i.e. number of problem instances solved in a single man-hour of playing). The attractiveness is an expression of how much people like the game, more rigidly: how much man-hours of playing we could possibly harness. The attractiveness is determined with two aspects of a SAG: ability to *attract* and ability to *keep* the attention of the player. It is also important to track the ability of the game to spread virally (since we have no capacity to propagate the game in a greater scale). We conducted a player survey, in which we asked [5]:

- If and how the players understood the game principles and purpose (the ability of attracting the attention is strongly influenced by this).
- If they would play again (the ability to keep player's attention) and if they would recommend it to a friend (effectively the ability of viral spreading).
- If they were somehow convinced with the "greater good" of the game to play it.

Results of the questionnaire showed that the game is not self-explaining enough (many players answered that they needed to consult the manual or the game author in order to understand the game). This means the lack of ability to attract attention. On the other hand, the game was liked by 80 % of players and almost one third of them would spread it virally. Also the interesting result is that 1/6 of the players were actually convinced by the game purpose to play (which supports the notion that the game purpose has to be known to the players). Results of the questionnaire leaves the attraction problem open, but encourages to continue on this project.

8.2 PexAce

From the SAG design point of view, the PexAce is a demonstration of a game, which motivates players to create useful artifacts but does not require immediate evaluation of these artifacts after the game session to provide score. It therefore can remain single-player and require no control data set for bootstrapping as other games need to [3, 6]. In addition, the PexAce-Personal modification of the game applies an unique player motivation—option to use the "purposeful output" (the image tags) of the game for himself. Moreover, with PexAce, we demonstrate the potential of using the information about player expertise to improve quality of its output metadata. As well as other games, PexAce too was under threat of malicious player behavior. Thus we were also forced to improve the game in this way, mixing the prevention with a posteriori cheating detection.

8.2.1 Helper Artifacts: A Novel Approach for Artifact Validation

Being a semantics acquisition game, the PexAce has an unusual scoring mechanism which is not dependent on the actual quality of the artifacts (image annotations) that player is creating within the game. In fact, the player can completely omit the annotations and rely on his memory only. He is scored only according to the time he need for the game and (more importantly) the number of flips he makes. Nevertheless, creating meaningful annotations may help him a lot in improving his score, so the player is usually motivated to do it. And he does it.

The game can stay single-player this way. Its scoring function is objective, exact, transparent and can be executed automatically. This greatly boosts the game in its early stages of deployment—there is no cold start problem regarding insufficient number of players wanting to play or a need for an existing validation data set. And still, even if the score is not computed out of the quality of the artifacts created, the players create them and they create them in quality (they truly describe the given images), because otherwise, they would not be useful for them.

This is a new method of artifact validation in SAGs which we call the *helper artifacts*. It is based on a principle that in order to build a SAG, we firstly create a non-purpose game (or take one existing game, such as Concentration) with its own scoring system. Then we add new features to the game that would enable players to (slightly) ease the overcoming of the obstacles in the game (e.g. adding a tool for labeling the images for aiding their memory). The only condition left is that the actions (or artifacts they create) that the players are helping themselves with, must also be useful outside the game.

We believe that this concept can be used widely for SAGs. If we consider the domain of resource description only, a memory-based games similar to PexAce could be devised for other types of resources (video streams, audio). Also, not only textual artifacts could be product of player helping themselves: instead they can draw sketches on the screen or record a voice through audio input devices.

An interesting option for using the helper artifacts may also be to restrict their set of possible values to enable categorization. For example, in a hypothetical "music card, PexAce-like game", the only possible options to annotate the cards would be different moods that can be experienced during music listening.

The use of helper artifacts within a game is flexible which has a potential in balancing the game. The game can be either heavily "populated" with them or use them only sparsely. The moving between these extremes is easily done: you can limit the player by number of helper artifacts he can create. This may prove important in case we discover that players feel that the game is not very attractive because "it looks like a work" or "it is boring". In such case a SAG based on some other artifact validation method may prove hard to be improved. However, with helper artifacts, one can simply reduce their presence in the game and give more weight to other (potentially more attractive) features of the game.

8.2.2 Apparent Purpose and Motivation to Play PexAce

8.2.2.1 PexAce for General Images

The PexAce *does not encapsulate its purpose*. A player playing PexAce, who is aware of the image metadata concept may quickly recognize the "trick" the game is using to acquire the image annotations. After the game was deployed, several players reported that the game started to bore them after some point, when they realized they are just systematically annotating the images.

Nevertheless, many players have been engaged by the *competition*, which was provided through a ladder system. We subsequently devised two ladder schemes. In first one, for each game the player received some points which then accumulated in his total score. This however, rewarded mostly players that contributed most time to the game, which quickly led to discouragement of other players to participate in the competition.

Therefore, we modified the total score computation function: the best games (most score) that player played counted more than the rest (formally: the score gains were sorted and before summing, i-th score was multiplied by the i-th member of a hyperbolic scale). This modification enabled more rapid score gain for new players and rewarded players with better performance in the game. In practice, the players responded positively. Because from the absolute numbers perspective, reaching the top of the ladder appeared close for the mid-ranking players and therefore, many of them contributed much effort in the game, even though their real chances of reaching the top of the ladder were minimal.

Connected to the competitive aspect, there is always a possible incentive of *self-challenge*: the player always struggles to overdo himself ("gain more points in one game").

For many players of a general version of the game (general domain of images) a minor incentive for playing was imposed by enjoyment and exploration of new images (a pleasure of *discovery*). Sometimes, they were pausing the gameplay, simply enjoying the new images they have not seen before. We have not pursued this incentive further with the general of our game, but in a future deployment, one may consider using a specific types of images that people like and enjoy and need to be annotated. An example of such more specific, but still wide domain of images is the viral content, which is fun to interact with.

8.2.2.2 PexAce for Personal Images

The personal imagery metadata acquisition version of the game, the PexAce-personal represent quite a different setup of motivations to play it. The game allows to play with one's own images, which has several consequences regarding motivation:

The *competition* aspect is suppressed (yet still present). The competition is technically, still possible. Even if individual players play with completely different sets of images—the scoring scheme is the same. The player cannot help himself by uploading some special, easy-to-remember set of images to the game, he would struggle in remembering or describing them just as with a set of random, casual images. In fact, he only may make the game *harder* for himself (e.g. uploading some abstract images, similar images).

He may though cheat with an automated wrapper if he uploads some images that can be easily recognized by automated methods, even after the images are hashed (for example, loading solid bitmaps with different colors). Such cheating possibility is the true reason why we do not rely on the competitive aspect of the PexAce-personal. Due to the fact that participation on a consensus could not be measured (as much of the metadata is provided by solo players and validated other way), the a posteriori anti-cheating is also short handed. Therefore, we decided to remove the reason for cheating, the global score ladder.

This removes much of the competitive motivation to play. Not entire though: we still see the possibility to organize competition among social circles of the players (which is common in many social games on the Web). If the circles are based on a real social bonds, then the sense of fair play is much more greater and potential cheaters discouraged. The community can also watch over itself: the individual players may (from time to time) peer-review the annotations and images of their opponents and report abuses so they are visible to the community.

Much of the motivation in PexAce-Personal is done by other than competitive incentives. The first one is somewhat similar to the general version of the game, yet much stronger: *joy of viewing one's own images* (or images of one's social circle). It is the same incentive that motivates people to review their photo albums from time to time: they like to refresh and "replay" their memories. Secondly, there is a very important incentive why to play the PexAce-Personal: *working for one's own sake*, i.e. organizing one's own image repository with the metadata created in the game.

None of the latter two motivations can really be categorized using the SAG design aspects system we described in this work (categories social experience, self-challenge, competition and discovery), simply because they are not present in any other SAGs.

On the contrary, we claim them as a contribution to the SAG design field. No other SAG before has used this type of motivation. We believe that combining *working for one's own sake* with other types of gameplay motivations in a SAG may dramatically boost its potential. Of course, it limits the use only for certain domains resp. problems (e.g. multimedia resource description), but this is still very wide. Especially if we recognize that the artifacts produced by players under these conditions have better quality (as we have shown in the experiments).

8.2.3 Player Competences

In PexAce, we have also experimented with recognizing player competences and using them for improving the game's output.

8.2.3.1 Recognizing Competences: A General Motivation

SAG players are not equal in terms of their knowledge. Therefore, the value (of artifacts) they deliver differs according to the tasks they solve. In semantics acquisition, these differences are mostly apparent across domains (an expert on the classical music may perform bad in case of techno in a music tagging game). They are also present in more specific domains or even between individual tasks (the player might be able to identify one work of van Gogh and meanwhile completely mismatch some other). Ultimately, some tasks could be executed by only some players.

Of course, the performance of the player (by which we mean the quality and quantity of usable artifacts) is also influenced by his motivation, joy or entertainment that the gaming process provide (especially in case of SAGs). But, these factors are also (at least partially) determined by the task domain (e.g. the content the user is interacting with).

Therefore, assigning the players with "right" tasks may arguably improve the outcome of the crowdsourcing process. If the tasks are assigned randomly to the players, it causes the low quality of the process results [1], e.g. too general meta-data [2]. Despite that, only few works have been issued to address this problem [1].

8.2.3.2 Experiments with PexAce Logs

To learn about the potential of recognizing and using the player expertise information, we re-examined the logs of the PexAce and run several synthetic experiments. Their basic idea was to compute information about player's expertise, then use it for weighting the player term suggestions and see, whether this leads to higher quality results.

We firstly needed to define some measures to represent the degree of player's expertise for the game. We worked with two measures:

1. **Usefulness**, which was defined as a ratio of number of correct term suggestions made by the player to all of his suggestions. The "correct term" means a term positively validated against golden standard, resp. judge evaluation.
2. **Participation on the consensus** or the **consensus ratio**, i.e. ratio of number of suggestions made by player that were also suggested by someone else to all of the player's suggestions.

The first measure exactly matches the value of the player (from the game's purpose standpoint), but cannot be acquired without a golden dataset. We can use it in laboratory conditions to evaluate the players, but it would be impossible to measure it during a real game deployment, where no dataset is available. On the other hand, the *consensus ratio* can be measured upon game deployment. However, though it can be reasonably expected to correlate with true usefulness (after all, the mutual player artifact validation is based on it) a bias can be expected.

Having the measures defined, we were seeking answers to following questions:

1. How do the players of the game differ? How do they differ according to their usefulness and how according to the consensus ratio? How does the usefulness correlates with the consensus ratio?
2. Will it help the game purpose, if we start to weight player suggestions according to the player usefulness? Will it improve the output quality? Is it sufficient to use the consensus ratio only, or we need to seek other ways of acquiring information about expertise of the players (other measures)?

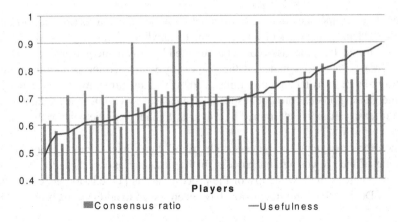

Fig. 8.1 The players of the PexAce (x-axis). A comparison of consensus ratios and usefulness for individual players. Surprisingly, there is only a partial correlation between the two measures

We took our game logs, which was basically a set of unique term suggestions for images (i.e. in a form *player-image-tag*). We have filtered out players with too few suggestions (less than 30 by the rule of thumb) resulting in 58 remaining players. We computed consensus ratio for each player. Using the golden standard we prepared in previous experiments, we computed usefulness for each player (see Fig. 8.1). Then, using the Pearson's correlation index, we computed the correlation of usefulness to the consensus ratio as 0.496. Such correlation is not high, as one would expect, but rather midway. Apparently, the consensus ratio bears a significant bias and does not always represent the true usefulness of the player. Even so, we tested whether it can help in increasing the quality of SAG output.

We have modified the original method of consensus tag filtering by introducing vote weights based on expertise. First, we used the usefulness values, second, the consensus ratio values. Both were originally numbers on the 0 to 1 interval so we directly use them as weight values. At the same time, we set up a *threshold* parameter, which was used to compute whether a consensus was or was not reached: if the sum of all suggestions (weights) suggesting the same tag to same images was higher than a threshold, the tag was accepted, otherwise not. We initially guessed the optimal threshold value as a doubled average usefulness value of the dataset (which was 0.7), however, we run the experiment multiple times with different thresholds.

Using the weighting methods, we repeatedly filtered the final tags. Each time, we compared the tags with the golden standard, computing the output correctness. The results can be seen in the Fig. 8.2, where both approaches were compared with a baseline correctness which was achieved without the use of weighting. As we can observe in the graph, with the growing threshold (increasing strictness), the usefulness-based approach starts giving results significantly more correct. We can also see that the performance of the consensus ratio-based method also grows, but

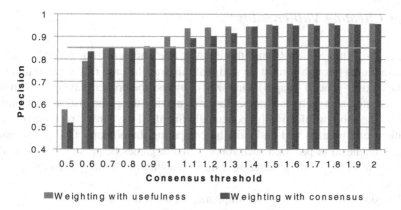

Fig. 8.2 The precision of the image tags produced by PexAce for different consensus thresholds:
(1) when usefulness is considered in suggestion weighting, (2) when consensus is considered in
suggestion weighting and (3) a baseline when no weighting is applied. We can see that using both
measures overdo the baseline, however, the consensus ratio is weaker, catching up with only higher
thresholds

much slower (i.e. requires higher strictness). Nevertheless, both approaches achieved
about 10 % increase of precision, which we consider very promising (see Fig. 8.2).

We consider these experiments a first step toward potentially heavy employment
of player expertise information in SAGs. The principles we used are general: they
can easily by adapted to other SAGs where mutual player artifact validation (offline
too) is used.

We have shown a significant improvement in PexAce's output quality, if player
expertise is considered, even if we use the consensus ratio, which can be measured
continuously throughout the game deployment (except the very early stages, when
not much logs exist). Also, the SAG can possibly use some gold standard dataset
tasks to test players skills, measure their usefulness directly and project it also onto
task instances on which no golden datasets exist.

Also, any external information on the player may be used, if it has an arguable
correlation with player's in-game skills. For example, if there are user interests user
models available, a multimedia resource description game or domain modeling game
can use it to decide what particular tasks would be useful for what player. By this,
we come to another dimension of the player expertise information: differentiating
between task types or task domains. For example, within a image annotation SAG
a player may prove skilled when describing cars and miserable when describing animals. We therefore see a large, yet "uncharted" research area comprising issues like:

- How to categorize task instances for game (how to create the categories and how
  to fill them)?
- How to assess the skills of players regarding these categories?
- How to effectively match the players to the tasks, particularly when there is not
  much manpower in the game?

8.2.4 Cheating Vulnerability

Just as the Little Search Game, the PexAce also suffered from several cheating vulnerabilities (though it must be said that this was the case of the game publicly deployed over general images). One way to bypass the proper playing, was to use an automated approach—a wrapper that was playing the game instead of a human player. The robot would simply sequentially flip all of the cards, "remember" their positions and bitmaps and find pairs by comparing the bitmaps. One of the game players managed to program such robot. It led to games being solved in virtually no time (naturally, without entering a single annotation), leading to almost perfect scores.

To reduce the use of robots we implemented the following:

1. We displayed slightly different images as pairs. This was achieved through slight blurring, pixel color mixing, toning, application of watermarks and slight card rotation. To a human eye, the images looked almost the same (and at the same time, the modifications were not disturbing) but for the simple pixel-by-pixel comparison, the task was suddenly impossible. Of course, we knew that some players might event come with more sophisticated methods of image comparison. However, no such attempts were made since.
2. We also applied the a posteriori cheating detection heuristics, which we used with the LSG. As indicators of dishonest gaming, we seek for co-occurrence of the following: (1) short gameplay times, (2) high ladder ranks, (3) a gameplay with no errors (repeated card flips) and (4) no created annotations for any of the images.

In case of PexAce, the combination of the reasonable prevention along with the application of a posteriori cheating detection (done permanently by a daemon script running on the game server) successfully distracted the dishonest players from abusing the game.

8.3 CityLights

The CityLights too is a game designed to be aware of the cold-start problems—it is a single player game. Its purpose is unique. Unlike other SAGs, this one do not create new metadata, but validate the existing ones. It is fueled by the existing (musical) *resource plus metadata dataset*, which the players are correcting and at the same time, getting score based on. Its design involves several notable features and also allows certain generalizations.

Several of our design aspects played a minor role in the design of the CityLights. The purposeful task of the game is to validate individual tag assignments to music resources. This is a naturally small task and we had no need in specially decomposing it. The tasks can also be considered *equally difficult*, resp. its difficulty depends more on the domain and quality of tags that are validated. Therefore, we could not really employ any gradual difficulty policy in game, except the fact that levels (sequences questions) for higher ranking players were composed from more tasks and therefore the player spent more time with them and put larger effort to acquire bonuses (which were awarded for no-mistake answering).

From all of our games, most effort was made to encapsulate the CityLights' purpose. Since a musical riddle is a common type of game and players did not have to type in any words, just use the cursor, most players have not realized that the game has some higher purpose (unless they read the game description). A solid effort was also made by devising an appealing graphical design of the game and also a simple metaphor of player wandering through the night city. These features too helped to encapsulate the purpose a bit.

The CityLights design also implicitly ruled out cheating threats. As a *prevention*, the game rules were set in a way that random player behavior would cause loosing the points in the game, instead of winning some—there was no other way of winning the game and gaining rank, than correctly answering questions. A hacking eventuality was also ruled out by using a thin client and moving all of the game's logic to the server side of the game.

8.3.1 Validation Games

The game is designed to minimize the cold-start problem via single-player. The single player nature of the game was enabled by the existence of the tag assignments featured in the game. The score in the game is inferred from the existing facts, however, these facts (assigned tags) only approximate the true solutions (correctly assigned tags) and the scoring is truly *independent* on the quality of artifacts. Therefore, we categorize the CityLights artifact evaluation mechanism as *approximative-algorithmic* scoring with a subsequent offline cross-player validation.

Still, this assignment does not fit so much, it is not an "approximative algorithmic evaluation", it only approximately scores the player while for the computation an existing metadata set is used, unusual to other SAGs.

We believe that CityLights may mark a new breed of semantics acquisition games, oriented towards validation of existing artifact assignments, e.g. descriptive metadata or term relationships. On abstract level, each of such games would operate with the same principle—a question—which of course could be incorporated into the game by various means and forms.

- The game constructs a question to the player with several possible answers. Both questions and answers could be any entities, relationships of which are to be validated. For example, in case of validating of descriptive metadata, the question can be represented by resource sample and answers by metadata, but it can be also other way around, e.g. the question may be some metadata sample and the answers some resources that can possibly match the question.

- One of the answers is based on an existing fact (or set of facts) that needs to be validated (though we also see a possibility to use some sort of multichoice question, the game designer might consider).
- The rest of the answers is wrong and therefore has to be"made up". For this, the very same dataset as the SAG aims to validate is the best source. From it, the entities can be drawn to form "wrong answers" having properties similar to the "right answer", making the game questions non-trivial and thus challenging.
- The player always acquires score, if he answers right and looses when he answers wrong (keeping the players from wrong guessing).
- The resulting game logs are then handled analogously to the CityLights. Each fact that needs to be validated receives a *support* value which is increased or lowered according to the behavior of the players. If they make mistakes provided with a fact, than this fact's support decreases and vice versa.

8.3.2 Game Aesthetics in CityLights

The CityLights attracts player by several types of game aesthetics. Primarily it is competition (trough ladder system) and self-challenge (through longer term goals). Secondarily, the game also provides sensation (sense-pleasure from hearing the music) and discovery (exploring new music).

A major role in game aesthetics is played by the game's scoring system. In the CityLights the player gains or looses points in several occasions during his journey through the city:

- At the start of the game, the player gains an initial number of points (so he is able to bet them).
- For each correct guess the player gains a *major* number of points, or looses them upon incorrect guess. He sets the height of the gain/loose as a bet. In our experiments, we used two possible bet height options (one being a twice as high as the other) to keep the game simple for players.
- The player looses if his score drops to zero, so he initial number of points is sufficient to make several unsuccessful guesses in a row.
- In the end of the game, the player gains a *major* number of extra points (the higher bet value), if he finished the game without making a mistake.
- For each bought tag, the player looses a *minor* number of points. This number is significantly lower than numbers of points featured in the bets (in our experiments, we used one tenth). The motivation to this is that even after the repeated tag buying (e.g. the player buys maximum additional tags to more choices), the correct answering still pays of, though with lower point gain. The tag buying, as well as bet height, gives the player some space to develop his tactics, which makes the game more interesting to him (he may, for instance, count on getting the bonus points at the end of the game).

- For explicit tag rule-out, the player gains *minor* number of points (same as with tag buying). This gain is always constant, regardless of how many tags the player rules out. As we have described before, the main motivation for the player in this case, is the "investment into future".

Note that the scale of the point gains is not so important (for instance, the bet values 100 and 200 would work just as well as 500 and 1,000), the important is to keep the proportions between major and minor point changes so the minor game actions (tag buying, tag rule-outs) remain interesting for the player but do not overrun the main scoring "function" (the betting).

If the player successfully finishes a game, his remaining score points are saved and added to his total score, which is kept over time. Total score serves as a means for sorting the players to a ladder. However, as recommended by Luis von Ahn [6], the motivational effects of the ladders and scoring systems are better, if they are complemented with the "experience" and "player level" system, which originally emerged in the classical role-playing games, where player develops his personal avatar.

In an experience/level system, which we also employed in the CityLights, the score has a form of *experience* points, which indicate how much effort the player had invested in the game. Furthermore, each player has also a *level*, which indicates that he had reached a certain milestones. In a common case, the player reaches a next level after he gains a certain number of experience points. The level is then the primary mean of comparing of the players and has several advantages:

1. The milestones represent a longer term challenges (in comparison to the finishing of the game) and motivate players to play more.
2. The comparison of players more understandable with small numbers of level values than large numbers of experience values.
3. New players with low levels feel more confident to reach the high ranking players. This is because the relation between the experience and level increase is logarithmic (with the linear experience increase, the level rises on the logarithmic basis) and therefore, even the players with extremely high experience seem to be relatively close to the new players in the ladder, which motivates the new players for further playing.
4. The minor differences in the experience counts nivelize groups of players to one level and by this further encourages their competition as every player wants to distinguish himself by higher level than others have.

The experience and level system of the CityLights follows the principles described above. The player engages it through multiple ladders and level gauge in the main menu of the game application (see Fig. 8.3). The level gauge (top-right corner) indicates, how much experience he needs for reaching the next level. The three ladders (overall, monthly and weekly) propose other short and long term challenges for the player ("be the first this month").

Fig. 8.3 The CityLights menu interface, featuring ladders for the player (*right*) and his level gauge (*top-right corner*)

8.3.3 Player Competences Expressed Through Confidence

As we have demonstrated with the PexAce, it has a positive impact on a SAG output, if the game resp. the artifact evaluation mechanism "is aware" of player's competences and uses them weight their suggestions. The CityLights too operates with the information about the player competences but in a different way: it assesses this information for each question and player separately—through betting system.

In the game, prior to answering a question, the player bets some of his points. If he answers correctly, he doubles them, if the answer is wrong, he looses them. This is a notorious and popular principle of gambling and is present in many computer games too, where virtual credits are used instead of real money.

However, in CityLights, the betting also serves another important purpose: Through the height of his bet, the player implicitly tells us, how confident he is about himself answering that question. And through his confidence, we can estimate his *competence* (or expertise) for that particular question. This is based on a natural assumption: if someone is confident to do something, he *probably* is also skilled at it. There is of course a counterargument: what if someone is notoriously overconfident about his skills? The answer is that from a global (SAG) view, only a part of players acts like that and the overall outcome is still good. Another answer is in the immediate feedback and small "iterations": the game quickly and repeatedly punishes for fails (which will come with lower player skill) and overconfident players quickly recognize their true skills.

And so, the confidence information is transformed to suggestion weights. In City-Lights, we used only two possible numbers of points per bet (one being a double of another). We then directly used them as coefficients in tag *support* delta computation.

We consider the confidence mechanism as another way of using the information about player's expertise in SAGs. We find it very viable for SAGs as it possess several interesting features:

- Betting is an attractive game feature that many game players appreciate.
- It can easily be incorporated to almost any game. It is simply a matter of prompting a player to place bet on action he is about to commence (whatever it may me).
- It is a system that support itself, it requires no external information.
- The system starts to work instantly with a new player, it does not require a longer observance of the player (such as with the consensus ratio measurement).
- Perspectively, the system can be used track also long term information on the player's expertise. If for example, we had game tasks with known categories (e.g. by sub-domain), we could measure longer term average confidence of the player for each category, possibly exploring his "effectiveness" for only some of them.

References

1. Chiou, C.L., Hsu, J.Y.J.: Capability-aligned matching: improving quality of games with a purpose. In: The 10th International Conference on Autonomous Agents and Multiagent Systems—Volume 2, AAMAS '11, pp. 643–650. International Foundation for Autonomous Agents and Multiagent Systems, Richland, SC (2011)
2. Roman, D.: Crowdsourcing and the question of expertise. Commun. ACM **52**, 12–12 (2009)
3. Seneviratne, L., Izquierdo, E.: An interactive framework for image annotation through gaming. In: Proceedings of the International Conference on Multimedia Information Retrieval, MIR '10, pp. 517–526. ACM, New York, NY, USA (2010)
4. Šimko, J., Tvarožek, M., Bieliková, M.: Creation of games with a purpose as tools for knowledge acquisition: Little google game. Znalosti 2011 (In Slovak) (2011)
5. Šimko, J., Tvarožek, M., Bieliková, M.: Semantics discovery via human computation games. Int. J. Semantic Web Inf. Syst. **7**(3), 23–45 (2011)
6. von Ahn, L., Dabbish, L.: Designing games with a purpose. Commun. ACM **51**(8), 58–67 (2008)

Chapter 9
Looking Ahead

Abstract The crowdsourcing and semantics acquisition games were with us for almost a decade. They helped solving many human intelligence tasks and attracted many researchers and practitioners. They demonstrated their potential, but also revealed weak points, among other, the inefficient incentives. As a meta-problem, the lack of holistic design methodology is still actual. Yet, we see the brighter future for the SAG field (as well as for the crowdsourcing in general), because of the constant progress of the humankind towards reducing the needs for manual work and leaving capacities for "mind labor".

We have shown that semantics acquisition happens to be the most crucial part of working with semantics. Although much effort has been done in automated semantics acquisition, there is still a need for human labor to complement it. The question on how to engage the people to participate in this process is still open. A large family of approaches—based on crowdsourcing—has been able to address the issues of costs and quantity demands, but for a price of uncertain quality of delivered results. The crowdsourcing approaches thrive to motivate their workers by alternative motivational factors, optimize the labor deployment and attempts to acquire more specific metadata.

In particular, we reviewed much of the current state of the art of crowdsourcing games and semantics acquisition games (SAGs) in particular. For almost a decade the crowdsourcing games were an agenda for a constantly growing number of researchers (Pe-Than et al. reported over hundred of works [2]). We have seen crowdsourcing game performing jobs for various domains, often connected to semantics acquisition (their deployment outside semantics acquisition domain is sparse, but perspectively not restricted). In many cases the SAGs proved that they are able to motivate their players to contribute their brain-power. On the other hand, the field of SAG design is still only loosely conceptualized and we lack a holistic SAG design methodology.

SAG design has also been evolving. SAGs initially emerged with one dominant design principle: a two player game where players "control" each other. Later other paradigms pursuing single player schemes appeared, though the multiplayer variant prevails dominant to this day. SAGs comprise several forms of aesthetics:

J. Šimko and M. Bieliková, *Semantic Acquisition Games*,
DOI: 10.1007/978-3-319-06115-3_9,
© Springer International Publishing Switzerland 2014

competition, socialization, self-challenge, discovery which are found in regular games. They also inherited drawbacks of regular games: the malicious player behavior, with which they also needed to deal with.

Many issues remain open. For example, there are still challenges in quality control of player outputs. One of the possible research directions regarding this are methods taking into account the different skill levels of individual players. Only recently, the SAG designers started to think about working with player expertise information, which is more common in general crowdsourcing.

The SAGs proved very strong, when the content they work with is attractive to players (e.g. multimedia), but lack breath when they are working with texts (a case especially for domain modeling games). The lack of ability to attract players is the main reason why many SAGs are de facto dead projects, although their design appear sound. It is often caused by lack of the "purpose encapsulation", often criticized by players who perceive SAGs as type of work, others simply refuse to be "outsourced for free". It is unfortunate, but unless a much deeper insight into the crowdsourcing game aesthetics is given by game design researchers and practitioners, the SAGs (many of which are created by people from the "target problem domains", i.e. not game designers) will continue to have the attractiveness issues.

From a researcher's perspective, there is yet more one drawback regarding SAGs: there is no regularly established and internationally accepted forum dedicated to SAGs. The research community around SAGs is instead spread among much wider crowdsourcing community, or distributed across problem domains to which the purposes of the games belong (e.g. ontology building, image annotation, image acquisition in context of geo-space, music information retrieval).

9.1 Brighter Future

Nevertheless, we see the future of the field (SAG and general crowdsourcing) as optimistic. As anecdotally envisioned by Luis von Ahn, in the future, every manual task will be done by machines. The people would then be split into two classes: those, who will create the SAGs and those, who will only "eat, sleep and play"[1] them, solving the human intelligence tasks, which machines won't be able to solve.

Although this is vastly exaggerated, a more realistic point can be made out of it. The overall technological advances of human civilization, automation of manual tasks etc. may potentially relieve more and more human laborers. On the other hand, unless a major breakthrough is made in a field of practical artificial intelligence, there will still be an increasingdemand for performing human intelligence tasks (e.g. programming the manual workers). Hence, the crowdsourcing will be a convenient option for saturating the tensions. We believe, that crowdssourcing with all its methods, will make an efficient endeavor.

---

[1] A phrase acronym of which gave a name to Ahn's most renown game, the ESP.

We do not yet know, which of the paradigms of the crowdsourcing will be dominant in such world, be it either SAGs, micro-payment mechanisms such as Amazon Mechanical Turk or something else. We believe, that more probable case is the second. "Turking" is much more straightforward to prepare, covers (even today) much more domains (e.g. business intelligence) that SAGs have not reached yet. It also provides money to the contributors—a very strong incentive (some of the available crowdsourcing tasks are comparable to low paying jobs in terms of financial income for the contributor). Many payment-based crowdsourcing platform users complement their primary salaries with "crowdsourcing money", although they usually need another motivation to participate. But, the money are also the downside: the task owners have limited budgets and would appreciate another type of motivations, such as entertainment provided by SAGs. SAGs will also have an advantage of engaging potential contributions during time they consider "free", something that "work-like" approach would have problem with.

In any way, the steady rise of crowdsourcing utilization will be significantly fueled by today's almost ubiquitous availability of personal computing devices, especially mobile ones. While in the past, the crowdsourcing approaches heavily relied on the Web environment, today they too start adapt to major paradigm shift to mobile devices. The potential is clear: unlocking of many hours of "availableness" of the users (e.g. traveling, waiting).

Micro-payment schemes have the advantage here, some vendors already provide mobile morphs of their original web applications.[2] For SAGs, this transition may take more time and effort: a game must be carefully adjusted to different features of the mobile interface. Some of the SAGs designs may even be infeasible, for example because they require large display or heavily rely on typing, which is not a popular activity of the today's mobile device users (e.g. our PexAce). On the other hand, many currently existing SAGs may be transformed to mobile versions straightforwardly (e.g. our CityLights). Some new SAGs are even exclusive to the mobile devices— they are used for harvesting real world geographical information [1].

References

1. Chen, L.J., Syu, Y.S., Chen, H.C., Lee, W.C.: The design and evaluation of task assignment algorithms for gwap-based geospatial tagging systems. Mob. Netw. Appl. **17**(3), 395–414 (2012)
2. Pe-Than, E.P.P., Goh, D.H.L., Lee, C.S.: A typology of human computation games: an analysis and a review of current games. Behav. Inf. Technol. **33**, 1–16 (2014)

---

[2] http://radar.oreilly.com/2009/10/mechanical-turk-on-iphone-provides-work-for-refugees.html